Hit List:

Frequently Challenged Young Adult Titles; References to Defend Them

prepared by

The Intellectual Freedom Committee
Young Adult Services Division

Young Adult Services Division
American Library Association
1989

Published by the Young Adult Services Division
American Library Association
50 East Huron Street
Chicago, IL 60611-2795

ISBN: 0-8389-7329-9

Printed in the United States of America.

Table of Contents

Introduction

The first edition of the *Hit List: Frequently Challenged Young Adult Titles; References to Defend Them* has been more than two years in development. The members of the committee hope that the information gathered here will provide timely assistance to librarians by making easily available complete citations to reviews and other critical materials for twenty of the most frequently challenged books of interest or appeal to young adult readers.

The committee would like to thank Judith Krug and the staff of the Office for Intellectual Freedom (OIF) for sharing with us their records of challenges reported to the OIF. The twenty titles chosen for this first effort were selected because they were among the most frequently challenged titles according to OIF records. Further documentation of challenges to these titles was found in the 1986-1987 annual report of The People for the American Way, *Attacks on the Freedom to Learn*.

Members of this committee would be glad to hear from other librarians who have collected other resources which they have used successfully to defend any of these twenty titles. We also solicit your comments on the materials cited here, and your suggestions for improvements to this publication.

Please send all comments to:

YASD Intellectual Freedom Committee
c/o Young Adult Services Division
American Library Association
50 East Huron Street
Chicago, IL 60611

Go Ask Alice

Anonymous

Englewood Cliffs, NJ: Prentice-Hall, 1971. LC: 74-159446. ISBN: 0-13-357111-4.

Annotation

Alleged to have been based on an actual diary of a teenage girl who became a drug addict and died of an overdose, *Go Ask Alice* has been a controversial title throughout the seventeen years since it first appeared. It describes how Alice first became fascinated with and entangled in the drug culture after her family moved away from their hometown and she had difficulty adjusting to a new school and making new friends. She is excited by the intensity of the "highs" she experiences when tripping on drugs, and terrified of the dangers involved.

The book, written in diary form, presents first-hand the life of the West Coast drug culture of the late 1960s-early 1970s. Alice and a friend run away from home, hitch their way from one hippie commune to the next, become prostitutes to support their drug habits, and run the gamut of disease, degradation and despair.

Alice makes several attempts to free herself from drugs, returns home and receives care and support from her parents, who do everything they can to help her. The book makes it clear that overcoming drug addiction involves more than the detoxification process---it means forsaking all your former friends and acquaintances and completely renouncing old habits and hangouts. Although Alice tries to stay straight, she fails to break contact with the "dopers" and is lured back into the vicious cycle of addiction.

The strength of the book is its honesty in depicting both the allure and the horror of drug addiction, and the difficulty in breaking free not only from the physical addiction to the drugs but also the emotional and psychological dependence of the drug culture lifestyle. Alice's parents are depicted as loving and caring. wanting beyond everything to help their daughter, supportive of her efforts to break free. The explicit language, frank descriptions of sexual experiences, and detailed accounts of good and bad "trips," present readers with the consequences of drug addiction and prod them to draw their own conclusions.

The conclusion of the book, in which Alice seems to be making progress in overcoming her problems, is deliberately left open-ended. An epilogue reveals that Alice is found dead of a drug overdose, which may have been accidental, or deliberately administered, or even suicide. This epilogue encourages readers to speculate on Alice's state of mind, and to think about what they have just read.

A "made-for-television" film of the story was made by Metromedia Productions and aired on ABC-TV on January 24, 1973. Directed by John Korty and produced by Gerald I. Isenberg, it featured Jamie Smith Jackson as Alice and William Shatner as Sam.

Examples of Recent Challenges

Removed from school libraries in Kalamazoo, Michigan (1974), of Levittown, New York (1975), Saginaw, Michigan (1975), Eagle Pass, Texas (1977), Trenton, New Jersey (1977), North Bergen, New Jersey (1980), due to "objectionable" language and explicit sex scenes.

Challenged at the Marcellus, New York school district (1975), Ogden, Utah school district (1979), Safety Harbor, St. Petersburg, Florida Middle School library (1982), where written parental permission was required to check out the title.

Challenged at the Osseo school district in Brooklyn Park, Minnesota (1983) when a school board member found the book's language "personally offensive." Challenged in the Pagosa Springs, Colorado schools (1983) because a parent objected to the "graphic language, subject matter, immoral tone, and lack of literary quality found in the book."

Challenged at the Rankin County, Mississippi school district (1984) because it is "profane and sexually objectionable." Challenged at the Gwinnett County, Georgia Middle School (1986) by members of Citizens for Excellence in Education because of "filth, profanities and perversities." Challenged at the Central Gwinnett, Georgia High School library (1986) because "it encourages students to steal and take drugs."

The Gainesville, Georgia Public Library (1986) prohibits young readers from checking out this book along with forty other books. The books, on subjects ranging from hypnosis and drug abuse, to breast-feeding and sexual dysfunction, are kept in a locked room.

Removed from the middle school library in Kalkaska, Michigan (1987) because the book contained "objectionable language and encouraged sexual experimentation."

Sources: Office for Intellectual Freedom, American Library Association; and The People for the American Way.

Reviews

Best Sellers. 32:263 (9/1/72). ISSN: 0005-0019.

Booklist. 68:611 (3/15/72); 68:663 (4/1/72). ISSN: 0006-7385.

Catholic Library World. 43:219 (12/71). ISSN: 0008-820X.

Christian Science Monitor. 63:B6 (11/11/71).

Commonweal. 95:190 (11/19/71). ISSN: 0010-5330.

Kirkus Reviews. 39:776 (7/15/71). ISSN: 0042-6598.

Library Journal. 97:1174 (3/15/72); 97:1884 (5/15/72). ISSN: 0363-0277.

New York Times Book Review. Part II:42 (11/5/72). ISSN: 0028-7806.

Publishers Weekly. 201:80 (3/27/72). ISSN: 0000-0019.

Times Literary Supplement. (9/1/72). ISSN: 0307-6614.

Articles

Peck, Richard. "In the country of teenage fiction." *American Libraries* 4:204-207 (4/73). ISSN: 0002-9769.

Recommended Reading Lists

Best Books for Young Adults, 1971. Young Adult Services Division, American Library Association.

Carlsen, G. Robert. *Books and the Teenage Reader, 2nd Revised Ed.* New York: Harper and Row, 1980. pp. 71-72. LC: 78-2117. ISBN: 0-06-010626-3.

Dreyer, Sharon Spredemann. *The Bookfinder: A Guide to Children's Literature About the Needs and Problems of Youth Aged 2-15.* 3v. Circle Pines, MN: American Guidance Service, dates vary. v.1 (1977) #27. LC: 78-105919. ISBN: 0-913476-45-5.

Public Library Catalog, 8th Ed. Ed. by Gary L. Bogart and John Greenfieldt. New York: H. W. Wilson, 1984. p. 365. LC: 84-3508. ISBN: 0-8242-0702-5.

Senior High School Library Catalog, 13th Ed. New York: H. W. Wilson, 1987. LC: 87-7377. ISBN: 0-8242-0755-6.

Your Reading: A Booklist for Junior High and Middle School Students. Ed. by Jane Christensen. Committee on the Junior High and Middle School Booklist. Urbana, IL: National Council of Teachers of English, 1983. p. 641. LC: 83-17426. ISBN: 0-8141-5938-9.

Deenie

By Judy Blume

Scarsdale, NY: Bradbury Press, 1973. LC: 73-80197. ISBN: 0-878-88061-5.

Annotation

Beautiful twelve-year-old Deenie Fenner has a hard time coping with her desire to be liked and liked by everybody else in her crowd and her mother's ambition for her to pursue a successful modeling career. But when she is diagnosed as having adolescent idiopathic scoliosis (curvature of the spine) and finds out that she will have to wear a back brace for four years to correct it, life as she has known it comes to an abrupt halt. Deenie is panic-stricken at the thought of becoming a "handicapped" person. After so many years of emphasizing the absolute importance of physical beauty, her mother doesn't know how to cope with the idea of a "deformed" daughter either, and cannot believe that this is happening to them. Her parents, who have been so supportive, are suddenly "not there" for Deenie.

Deenie must look inside herself for the strength to face this situation. In spite of many difficulties, she learns to come to terms with herself and her disability. She also learns that she does not have to be "perfect" to survive.

Masturbation is mentioned twice, as Deenie casts about for ways to comfort herself and counteract the stress she is feeling. At one point Deenie touches herself and finds that it makes her feel better. "Myths" about masturbation and its effects are explained through the character of an understanding gym teacher. Deenie is surprised and relieved to discover that her feelings and actions are normal and part of growing up.

Examples of Recent Challenges

Removed from the Utah State Library bookmobile (1980) because the book contains "the vilest sexual descriptions" and if given to "the wrong kid at the wrong time (would) ruin his life."

Removed from the Gilbert, Arizona elementary school libraries (1980), and ordered that parental consent would be required for students to check out this title from the junior high school library.

Challenged in Orlando, Florida (1982); challenged in the Cotati-Rohnert Park, California school district (1982) because the novel allegedly undermines parental moral values.

After the Minnesota Civil Liberties Union sued the Elk River, Minnesota School Board (1983), the board reversed its decision to restrict this title to students who have written permission from their parents.

Banned, but later restricted to students with parental permission at the Peoria, Illinois school district libraries (1984), because of its strong sexual content and language, and alleged lack of social or literary value.

Removed from the Hanover, Pennsylvania school district's elementary and secondary school libraries (1984) but later placed on a "restricted shelf" at middle school libraries because the book was "indecent and inappropriate."

Challenged at the Casper, Wyoming school libraries (1984). Challenged as profane, immoral and offensive, but retained in the Bozeman, Montana school libraries (1985).

Banned from district elementary school libraries in Gwinnett County, Georgia (1985) as "inappropriate."

Returned to the elementary and junior high school library shelves in Clayton County, Georgia (1985) after school officials determined that the book is appropriate for young readers.

Source: The Office for Intellectual Freedom, American Library Association.

Reviews

Booklist. 70:444 (12/15/73). ISSN: 0006-7385.

Center for Children's Books Bulletin. 27:123 (4/74). ISSN: 0008-9036.

Commonweal. 99:215 (11/23/73). ISSN: 0010-5330.

Kirkus Reviews. 41:965 (9/1/73). ISSN: 0042-6598.

Library Journal. 99:1471 (5/15/74). ISSN: 0363-0277.

Mother Jones. 5:60 (1/80). ISSN: 0362-8841.

New York Times Book Review. (11/4/73). ISSN: 0028-7806.

Psychology Today. 8:132 (9/74). ISSN: 0033-3107.

Publishers Weekly. 204:97 (10/8/73). ISSN: 0000-0019.

Teacher. 91:111 (1/74) and 92:116 (2/75). ISSN: 0148-6578.

Standard Reference Sources

Children's Literature Review. Detroit: Gale Research Company, 76. v.2 pp. 15-19. LC: 75-34953. ISBN: 0-8103-0078-8.

Contemporary Authors. Detroit: Gale Research Company, 1978. v.29 pp. 29-32R, 72. LC: 62-52046. ISBN: 0-8103-0035-4.

Contemporary Authors: New Revision Series. Detroit: Gale Research Company, 1984. v.13 pp. 59-62. LC: 81-640179. ISBN: 0-8103-1942-X.

Contemporary Literary Criticism. Detroit: Gale Research Company, 1980. v.12 pp. 44-48. LC: 76-38938. ISBN: 0-8103-0122-9; 1984. v.30 pp. 20-25. LC: 76-38938. ISBN: 0-8103-4404-1.

Current Biography Yearbook/1980. Ed. by Charles Moritz. New York: H. W. Wilson, 1981. pp. 17-20. LC: 40-27432. ISSN: 0084-9499.

Fourth Book of Junior Authors and Illustrators. Ed. by Doris De Montreville. New York: H. W. Wilson, 1978. pp. 46-47. LC: 87-115. ISBN: 08-8242-0568-5.

Something About the Author. Ed. by Anne Commire. Detroit: Gale Research Company. v.2 pp. 31-32; v.31 pp. 28-34. LC: 70-127412. ISBN: 0-8103-0057-5. ISSN: 0276-816X.

Stott, Jon. *Children's Literature from A-Z*. New York: McGraw-Hill, 1984. pp. 40-43. LC: 84-4425. ISBN: 0-07-061791-0.

Twentieth Century Children's Writers, 2nd Ed. New York: St. Martin's Press, 1983. LC: 83-40062. ISBN: 0-312-8241-9.

Who's Who in America 1987-88. 139th Ed. New York: St. Martin's Press, 1987. LC: 87-16933. ISBN: 0-312-002636-X.

Articles

"ACLU appeals *Deenie* ban." *School Library Journal* 32:11 (12/85). ISSN: 0362-8930.

"Author! Author! Meet Judy Blume." *Teen* 24:65 (7/80). ISSN: 0040-2001.

"Author Judy Blume wins numerous prizes." *School Library Journal* 30:25-26 (9/83). ISSN: 0362-8930.

Bachemin, M. A. "Meet your favorite author, Judy Blume." *Teen* 26:30+ (10/82). ISSN: 0040-2001.

"Blume books restricted in Peoria, Ill.; five titles banned in Hanover, Pa." *School Library Journal* 31:7 (1/1/85). ISSN: 0362-8930.

Bohning, Patricia and Ann Nauman. "Judy Blume: the lady and the legend." *Emergency Librarian* 14:17-20 (11-12/86). ISSN: 0315-8888.

"Censorship update." *School Library Journal* 29:9 (11/82). ISSN: 0362-8930.

Decter, Naomi. "Judy Blume's children." *Commentary* 69:65-67 (3/80). ISSN: 0010-2601.

Garvey, J. "Voice of Blume." *Commonweal* 107:392 (7/4/80). ISSN: 0010-3330.

Goldberger, J. M. "Judy Blume: target of the censor." *Newsletter on Intellectual Freedom* 30:57+ (5/81). ISSN: 0028-9485.

Miscellaneous Discussion

Lee, Betsey. *Judy Blume's Story* Minneapolis, MN: Dillon Press, 1981. LC: 81-12494. ISBN: 0-875-18209-7.

Awards and Prizes

Although Judy Blume has not received any awards or prizes for *Deenie*, a list of the prizes won by her other books appears in v.31 of *Something About the Author*. See **Standard Reference Sources.**

Recommended Reading Lists

Dreyer, Sharon Spredemann. *The Bookfinder: A Guide to Children's Literature About the Needs and Problems of Youth Aged 2-15*. 3v. Circle Pines, MN: American Guidance Service, dates vary. v.1 (1977) #88. LC: 78-105919. ISBN: 0-913476-45-5.

Junior High School Library Catalog, 4th Ed. Ed. by Gary L. Bogart and Richard H. Issacson. New York: H. W. Wilson, 1980. p. 390. LC: 80-53462. ISBN: 0-8242-0652-5.

Spirt, Diana L. *Introducing More Books; A Guide for the Middle Grades*. New York: R. R. Bowker, 1978. pp. 76-78. LC: 78-13490. ISBN: 0-8352-0988-1.

Your Reading: A Booklist for Junior High and Middle School Students. Ed. by Jane Christensen. Committee on the Junior High and Middle School Booklist. Urbana, IL: National Council of Teachers of English, 1983. p. 191. LC: 83-17426. ISBN: 0-8141-5938-9.

Forever

By Judy Blume

Scarsdale, NY: Bradbury Press, 1975. LC: 74-22850. ISBN: 0-02-711030-3.

Annotation

Katherine, the heroine of *Forever*, experiences turmoil, changes, romance and loss during the course of her senior year in high school. By the end of the year (and the story's conclusion) she has experienced and accepted both the pains and the pleasures of growth and has found a new level of maturity.

She has outgrown her relationship with her steady boyfriend, Michael, but the relationship is one she will remember and treasure, because of the experiences they shared---including her first sexual experience, always special no matter how inadequate.

The story contains specific descriptions of sexual acts and the language is explicit. Blume is attempting to describe, with honesty leavened by humor, what "first love" feels like at the moment it is experienced. She emphasizes also the responsibilities of both partners in a love affair by incorporating frank discussions of sexually transmitted diseases, masturbation, condoms and birth control methods. Katherine and Michael behave sensibly and take precautions to protect themselves.

Their relationship is not carried out in a state of blissful unawareness either. They are also asked to deal with peer pressure, suicide and the death of a loved one.

The affair ends gently, as Katherine and Michael move on in different directions. No one gets hurt and no one gets left behind. Blume has taken pains to show that love and happiness in human relationships is a process of continuing growth and change that has nothing to do with the fairy tale fantasy of "happily forever after."

A "made-for-television" film of *Forever* (under the same title) was produced by Roger Gimbel for EMI-TV Productions in 1978.

Examples of Recent Challenges

Challenged at the Midvalley Junior-Senior High School in Scranton, Pennsylvania (1982) because it contains "four-letter words and talked about masturbation, birth control and disobedience to parents."

Challenged at the Park Hill, Missouri South Junior High School library (1982) where it was housed on restricted shelves because the book promotes "the stranglehold of humanism on life in America."

Challenged at the Orlando, Florida schools (1982); the Akron, Ohio School District libraries (1983); challenged at the Howard-Suamico, Wisconsin High School (1983) because "it demoralizes marital sex."

Challenged and eventually moved from the Holdredge, Nebraska Public Library young adult section to the adult section (1984) because the "book is pornographic and does not promote the sanctity of life, family life."

Challenged at the Cedar Rapids, Iowa Public Library (1984) because it is "pornography and explores areas God didn't intend to explore outside of marriage."

Placed on a restricted shelf at Patrick County, Virginia school board (1986).

Challenged at the Campbell County, Wyoming school libraries (1986) because it is "pornographic" and would encourage young readers "to experiment with sexual encounters."

Challenged in Wright, Wyoming High School library (1986) for "condoning premarital sex, graphic sexual passages, and being pornographic." Removed from the Diamond Bar, California elementary school library (1986); challenged in the Moreno Valley, California high school library (1987) after a community group complained it was "obscene, profane, and sexually explicit."

Sources: The Office for Intellectual Freedom, American Library Association; and The People for the American Way.

Reviews

Booklist. 72:291 (10/15/75). ISSN: 0006-7385.

Center for Children's Books Bulletin. 29:106 (3/76). ISSN: 0008-9036.

English Journal. 65:90 (3/76); 66:64 (1/77); 67:90 (5/78). ISSN: 0013-8274.

Kirkus Reviews. 43:1136 (10/1/75). ISSN: 0042-6598.

Mother Jones. 5:60 (1/80). ISSN: 0362-8841.

New York Times Book Review. (12/28/75). ISSN: 0028-7806.

Publishers Weekly. 208:63 (8/18/75). ISSN: 0000-0019.

School Library Journal. 22:95 (11/75). ISSN: 0362-8930.

Times Literary Supplement. (10/1/76). ISSN: 0307-6614.

Standard Reference Sources

See the sources listed under citations for *Deenie.*

Articles

Forman, Jack. "Young adult books: 'Watch out for #1'." *Hornbook* 61:85 (1-2/85). ISSN: 0018-5078.

McNulty, Faith. "Children's books for Christmas." *New Yorker* 59:191 (12/5/83). ISSN: 0028-792X.

Maynard, Joyce. "Coming of age with Judy Blume." *New York Times Magazine* (12/3/78).

Thompson, Susan. "Images of adolescence: Part I." *Signal* 34:57-59 (1981). ISSN: 0037-4954.

Miscellaneous Discussion

Lee, Betsey. *Judy Blume's Story*. Minneapolis, MN: Dillon Press, 1981. LC: 81-12494. ISBN: 0-875-18209-7.

Awards and Prizes

Although Judy Blume has not received any awards or prizes for *Forever,* a list of the prizes won by her other books appears in v.31 of *Something About the Author.* See the **Standard Reference Sources** under *Deenie.*

Recommended Reading Lists

Books for You: A Booklist for Senior High Students. Ed. by Donald R. Gallo. Committee on the Senior High School Booklist. Urbana, IL: National Council of Teachers of English, 1985. p. 268. LC: 85-21666. ISBN: 0-8141-0363-4.

Campbell, Patricia J. *Sex Guides: Books and Films About Sexuality for Young Adults.* New York: Garland Publishing, Inc. 1986. pp. 334, 337, 340. LC: 85-45108. ISBN: 0-8240-8693-7.

Our Bodies, Ourselves; A Book By And For Women

By Boston Women's Health Collective

New York: Simon & Schuster, 1973. LC: 72-83220. ISBN: 0-671-21435-7.

The New Our Bodies, Ourselves; A Book by and for Women, 2nd Ed. New York: Simon & Schuster, 1985. LC: 84-5545. ISBN: 0-631-46087-0; 0-671-46088-9 (pb).

Annotation

Reference Sources for Small and Medium-sized Public Libraries describes this book as "a classic guide to women's health with information compiled from textbooks, medical journals, doctors, nurses and personal experiences. (It) covers sexuality and reproduction, nutrition, rape, venereal disease, birth control, abortion, childbearing, menopause and general health care for women."

The book is notable, not only for its frank presentation of content, but also for its emphasis on the importance of women having access to necessary information and being able to make informed decisions about their own lives, and to become responsible consumers of health care services. For young adult women this manual provides knowledge of how their bodies function, how to seek help, how to take care of themselves in a responsible manner, and how to avoid the consequences of acting in ignorance: illness, anxiety, premature sexual activity and pregnancy.

Examples of Recent Challenges

Removed from high school libraries in Townshend, Vermont (1975); Pinellas County, Florida (1975); Morgantown, West Virginia (1977); and Helena, Montana (1978).

Challenged in Amherst, Wisconsin (1982) due to its "pornographic" nature; Three Rivers, Michigan Public Library (1982) because it "promotes homosexuality and perversion."

Challenged at the William Chrisman High School in Independence, Missouri (1984) because the book is "filthy." The controversial feminist health manual was on a bookshelf in the classroom and was the personal property of the teacher.

Source: The Office for Intellectual Freedom, American Library Association.

Reviews

Choice. 22:1478 (6/85). ISSN: 0009-4978.

Library Journal. 98:405 (2/1/73). ISSN: 0363-0277.

Library Journal. 110:66 (3/15/85). ISSN: 0363-0277.

Nation.   240:473 (4/20/85).   ISSN: 0027-8378.

Newsweek.   81:94 (4/2/73).   ISSN: 0028-9604.

New York Times Book Review. (5/20/73).   ISSN: 0028-7806.

New York Times Book Review. (1/13/85).   ISSN: 0028-7806.

Saturday Review. 1:71 (3/73).   ISSN: 0361-1655.

Recommended Reading Lists

Best Books for Young Adults, 1976. Young Adult Services Division. Chicago: American Library Association, 1977. ISBN: 0-8389-5494-4.

Books for Public Libraries, 3rd Ed.   PLA Starter List Committee. Chicago: American Library Association, 1981.   p. 92.   LC: 81-14874. ISBN: 0-8389-0328-2.

Carlsen, G. Robert.   *Books and the Teenage Reader, 2nd Revised Ed.* New York: Harper and Row, 1980. pp. 26-27. LC: 78-2117. ISBN: 0-06-010626-3.

Public Library Catalog, 8th Ed. Ed. by Gary L. Bogart and John Greenfieldt. New York: H. W. Wilson, 1984. p. 357. LC: 84-3508. ISBN: 0-8242-0702-5.

Reference Sources for Small and Medium-sized Public Libraries, 4th Ed. Chicago: American Library Association, 1984.   p. 121. LC: 84-6513. ISBN: 0-8389-3293-2.

Senior High School Library Catalog, 13th Ed. New York: H. W. Wilson, 1987. LC: 87-7377. ISBN: 0-8242-0755-6.

Still Alive: Best of the Best, 1960-1974. Young Adult Services Division. Chicago: American Library Association, 1976.   ISBN: 0-8389-5477-4.

The Chocolate War; A Novel

By Robert Cormier

New York: Pantheon Books, 1974. LC: 73-15109. ISBN: 0-393-8280-5.

New York: Dell Publishing, 1974. ISBN: 0-490-94459-7 (pb).

Annotation

When Jerry Renault refuses to participate in the chocolate sale at his Catholic prep school, Trinity High, he becomes a hero to his schoolmates. But his refusal is a challenge that Brother Leon and the school's secret society, the Vigils, cannot abide. Slowly support for Renault falls away, and with the blessings of Brother Leon, Jerry is abandoned to the brutal revenge of the Vigils.

The Chocolate War has been criticized and challenged for its pessimism, harsh portrayal of adults and adult authority, and merciless picture of school life. It has been praised by reviewers and critics for its realism, literary style, and its underlying assumption that young adult readers are capable of critical thinking and able to form reasoned opinions about the world they inhabit. Cormier has been lauded for his use of language and symbolism. The *New York Times* has placed this novel on a par with Golding's *Lord of the Flies* and Knowles' *A Separate Peace*. Part of the novel's appeal to teen readers is its brutally honest picture of school life.

The novel's careful construction, terse readability and ability to provoke discussion has resulted in its being a recommended addition to many high school English curricula. *The Chocolate War* appears on many suggested reading lists, and remains one of the few young adult novels that respects the intelligence of its readers by offering them more than a happy ending and a simplistic solution.

Examples of Recent Challenges

Challenged and temporarily removed from the English curriculum in two Lapeer, Michigan high schools (1981) because of "offensive language and explicit descriptions of sexual situations in the book."

Removed from the Liberty High School in Westminster, Maryland (1982) due to the book's "foul language," portrayal of violence and degradation of schools and teachers.

Challenged at the Richmond, Rhode Island High School (1983) because the book was deemed "pornographic" and "repulsive."

Banned from the Richland Two School District middle school libraries in Columbia, South Carolina (1984) due to "language problems," but later reinstated for eighth-graders only.

Removed from the Lake Havasu, Arizona High School freshman reading list (1984). The school district board charged the Havasu teachers with failing to set good examples for students, fostering disrespect in the classroom, and failing to support the board.

Challenged at the Cornwall, New York High School (1985) because the novel is "humanistic and destructive of religious and moral beliefs and of national spirit."

Banned from the Stroudsburg, Pennsylvania High School library (1985) because it was "blatantly graphic, pornographic and wholly unacceptable for a high school library."

Challenged at Barnstable High School in Hyannis, Massachusetts (1986) because of the novel's profanity, "obscene references to masturbation and sexual fantasies," and "ultimately because of the pessimistic ending." The novel, complainants said, fostered negative impressions of authority, of school systems and of religious schools.

Challenged in the Bay County's four middle schools and three high schools in Panama City, Florida (1986) because it contains "profanity and sexual explicit passages."

Challenged at the Moreno Valley, California high school library as "obscene, profane, and sexually explicit."

Sources: The Office for Intellectual Freedom, American Library Association; and The People for the American Way.

Reviews

America. 130:350 (5/4/74). ISSN: 0002-7049.

American Libraries. 5:492 (10/74). ISSN: 0002-9769.

Center for Children's Books Bulletin. 27:173 (7/74). ISSN: 0008-9036.

English Journal. 62:112 (1/75). ISSN: 0046-6506.

Hornbook. 55:217 (4/79). ISSN: 0018-5078.

Kirkus Reviews. 42:371 (4/1/74). ISSN: 0042-6598.

Library Journal. 99:1450 and 1480 (5/74). ISSN: 0363-0277.

New Statesman. 89:694 (5/23/75). ISSN: 0039-0313.

New York Times Book Review. (12/1/74). ISSN: 0028-7806.

Publishers Weekly. 205:52 (4/15/74). ISSN: 0000-0019.

School Library Journal. 20:62 (5/74). ISSN: 0000-0035.

Times Literary Supplement. (4/4/75). ISSN: 0307-6614.

Washington Post Book World. (5/19/74). ISSN: 0006-7369.

Standard Reference Sources

Children's Literature Review. Detroit: Gale Research Company, 1987. v.12 pp. 114-139. LC: 75-34953. ISBN: 0-8103-03442.

Something About the Author. Detroit: Gale Research Company, 1986. v.45 pp. 59-65. LC: 72-2701. ISBN: 0-8103-2255-2.

Articles
ALAN Review. v.12 no.2 (Winter 1985). pp. 1-45. ISSN: 0882-2840.

Miscellaneous Discussion
Campbell, Patricia J. *Presenting Robert Cormier*. Boston: Twayne Publishers, 1985. LC: 85-9020. ISBN: 0-8057-8200-1.

"Looking backward: trying to find the classic young adult novel." *English Journal* 69:86-89 (9/80). ISSN: 0013-8274.

Probst, Robert E. *Adolescent Literature: Response and Analysis*. Columbus, OH: Charles E. Merrill Publishing Company, 1984. pp. 132-134. LC: 84-63534. ISBN: 0-675-20171-3.

Schwartz, Sheila. *Teaching Adolescent Literature*. Rochelle Park, NJ: Hayden Book Company, Inc. 1979. pp. 140-142. LC: 79-2042. ISBN: 0-8104-6036-X.

Awards and Prizes
ALAN Award 1983 for the body of his work, presented by the Assembly on Literature for Adolescents, National Council of Teachers of English.

Lewis Carroll Shelf Award 1979.

Media and Methods Maxi Award 1976 for best paperback, presented by *Media and Methods Magazine*.

Outstanding Books of 1974, presented by the *New York Times*.

Recommended Reading Lists
Best Books for Young Adults, 1974. Young Adult Services Division. Chicago: American Library Association, 1975. ISBN: 0-8389-5429-4.

"Best of the best, 1979." *School Library Journal* 26:63 (12/79). ISSN: 0000-0035.

Best of the Best, 1970-1983. Young Adult Services Division. Chicago: American Library Association, 1984. ISBN: 0-8389-5658-0.

Books for the Teen Age, 1975. New York Public Library.

Books for You: A Booklist for Senior High School Students. Ed. by Robert Small, Jr. Urbana, IL: National Council of Teachers of English, 1982. p. 197. LC: 82-8199. ISBN: 0-8141-0359-6.

Carlsen, G. Robert. *Books and the Teenage Reader, 2nd Revised Ed.* New York: Harper and Row, 1980. p. 77. LC: 78-2117. ISBN: 0-06-010626-3.

Gillespie, John T. *More Juniorplots; A Guide for Teachers and Librarians*. New York: R. R. Bowker, 1977. pp. 28-32.   LC: 77-8786. ISBN: 0-8352-1002-2.

Helbig, Alethea K. and Agnes Regan Perkins. *Dictionary of American Children's Fiction, 1960-1984: Recent Books of Recognized Merit*. New York: Greenwood Press, 1986. pp. 114-115.   LC: 85-24778. ISBN: 0-313-25233-5.

Junior High School Library Catalog, 5th Ed.   New York: H. W. Wilson, 1985. p. 361.   LC: 85-17934. ISBN: 0-8242-0720-3.

Outstanding Books for the College Bound: Fiction.   Young Adult Services Division.   Chicago: American Library Association. ISBN: 0-8389-5698-X.

Senior High School Library Catalog, 13th Ed.   New York: H. W. Wilson, 1987.   p. 859. LC: 87-7377. ISBN: 0-8242-0755-6.

Lord of the Flies

By William Golding

London: Faber & Faber, 1954.
New York: Coward, McCann, Geoghagen, 1962. LC: 65-51372.
ISBN: 0-698-10219-3.

Annotation

When the plane evacuating them from their school is shot down by enemy fire and crashes, a group of young boys is stranded on an uninhabited island. All of the adults on board are killed in the crash, and the boys are left to fend for themselves.

The older boys propose to elect a leader and establish a fair system for gathering food, building shelters and maintaining a signal fire to attract rescuers. They have every intention of behaving like reasonable men, imitating adults by discussing and voting on all their decisions as a group.

But these efforts to maintain order break down as fear of the unknown brings more primitive instincts to the surface. One of the strongest and most daring boys challenges the organization of the leaders. The group reverts to a mob, with the strongest boy imposing his will on the others. They obey out of fear and admiration of his prowess. The new "chief" sets up an idol or totem of a pig's head, which will magically protect them from their secret terrors as long as they obey it. He acts as spokesman and interpreter of the pig's commands. These commands become more and more irrational and savage, until the mob under the chief's command begins hunting down and killing the former leaders.

The last of these is only saved from a brutal death when a passing ship sees the smoke of the fires set to flush him out of hiding, and sends a boat ashore to investigate. The savage hunters revert to obedient school boys as soon as adult authority is reimposed.

The author implies however that the adults have only managed to disguise their own savagery, as the rescue ship turns out to be a navy destroyer on a mission to hunt down enemy ships.

Golding examines the nature of man and what constitutes civilized (redeemed) as opposed to savage (unredeemed) behavior. Some critics have interpreted Golding's fable as an attempt to show that man in his natural state, depending on his reason alone, cannot achieve a state of grace or salvation. His flawed nature will always bring him low. Only the intervention of God's saving grace can bring about redemption for the world.

In its style and substance, *Lord of the Flies* is remarkably like both Greek tragedy and the Biblical parable. Perhaps this accounts for the disquieting sensations which the book creates in its readers, who may not be prepared to discover either Aristotle's catharsis or the lost Garden of Eden, lurking beneath the trappings of a laconic adventure story.

Images and symbols are used with deliberate but ambiguous intent.   Nothing is what it first seems, and the story is open-ended: the readers must decide for themselves what lurks beneath the surface of society.

Examples of Recent Challenges

Challenged at the Dallas, Texas Independent School District high school libraries (1974); challenged at the Sully Buttes, South Dakota High School (1981); challenged at the Owen, North Carolina High School (1981] because the book is "demoralizing, inasmuch as it implies that man is little more than an animal."

Challenged at the Marana, Arizona High School (1983) as an inappropriate reading assignment. Challenged at the Olney, Texas Independent School District (1984) because of "excessive violence and bad language."

Challenged as optional reading for a tenth grade English class in Lincoln, Nebraska (1987) for its "portrayal of human nature, cruelty and violence, and because it does not represent the values of the home."

Sources: Office for Intellectual Freedom, American Library Association; and The People for the American Way.

Reviews

Library Journal. 80:1815 (9/1/55). ISSN: 0363-0277.

New Statesman. 48:370 (9/25/54). ISSN: 0028-6842.

New York Times Book Review. (10/23/55). ISSN: 0028-7806.

Saturday Review. 38:16 (10/15/55). ISSN: 0091-620X.

Times Literary Supplement. (10/22/54). ISSN: 0040-7895.

Standard Reference Sources

Contemporary Authors, New Revision Series. Ed. by Linda Metzger. Detroit: Gale Research Company, 1984. v.13 pp. 219-226.   LC: 81-640179. ISBN: 0-8103-1942-X.

Contemporary Literary Criticism. Editors vary.   Detroit: Gale Research Company, dates vary.

v.1	pp. 119-122.	(1973)	LC: 76-38938.	ISBN: 0-8103-0100-8.
v.2	pp. 165-169.	(1974)	LC: 76-38938.	ISBN: 0-8103-0102-4.
v.3	pp. 196-201.	(1975)	LC: 76-38938.	ISBN: 0-8103-0104-0.
v.8	pp. 249-250.	(1978)	LC: 76-38938.	ISBN: 0-8103-0114-8.
v.10	pp. 231-239.	(1979)	LC: 76-38938.	ISBN: 0-8103-0118-0.
v.17	pp. 157-181.	(1981)	LC: 76-38938.	ISBN: 0-8103-0107-5.
v.27	pp. 159-170.	(1984)	LC: 76-38938.	ISBN: 0-8103-4401-7.

Contemporary Novelists, 4th Ed. New York: St. Martin's Press, 1986. pp. 351-353. LC: 86-13904. ISBN: 0-312-16731-8.

Encyclopedia of World Literature in the Twentieth Century, Revised Ed. 4v. New York: Frederick Ungar Publishing Co., 1982. v.2 pp. 251-252. LC: 81-3357. ISBN: 0-8044-3136-1.

Who's Who, 1987-1988, 139th Ed. New York: St. Martin's Press, 1987. p. 670. LC: 4-16933. ISBN: 0-312-00236-X.

Articles

Baker, James R. "Interview with William Golding." *Twentieth Century Literature* 28:109-129 (Summer 1982). ISSN: 0041-462X.

Barr, Donald. "Should Holden Caulfield read these books?" *New York Times Book Review* 91:1+50-51 (5/4/86). ISSN: 0028-7806.

Bien, P. "Vision of a latter day modernist: William Golding's Nobel Prize." *World Literature Today* 58:185-188 (Spring 1984). ISSN: 0006-7431.

Egan, John M. "Golding's view of man." *America* 108:140-141 (1/26/63). ISSN: 0002-7049.

Green, M. "Distaste for the contemporary." *Nation* 190:451-454 (5/21/60). ISSN: 0027-8378.

Hynes, Samuel. "Novels of a religious man." *Commonweal* 71:673-675 (3/18/60). ISSN: 0010-3330.

Jones, R. "William Golding: genius and sublime silly-billy." *Virginia Quarterly Review* 60:675-687 (Autumn 1984). ISSN: 0042-675X.

Peter, John. "The fables of William Golding." *Kenyon Review* 19:577-592 (Autumn 1957). ISSN: 0163-075X.

Purvin, G. "Lord of the Flies---revisited." *Humanist* 44:31 (7-8/84). ISSN: 0018-7399.

Rexroth, Kenneth. "William Golding." *Atlantic Monthly* 215:96-98 (5/65). ISSN: 0004-6795.

Selby, K. "Golding's *Lord of the Flies*." *Explicator* 41:57-59 (Spring 1983). ISSN: 0014-4940.

Miscellaneous Discussion

Baker, James R. *William Golding: A Critical Study*. New York, St. Martin's Press, 1965. LC: 65-19796. ISBN: none listed.

Baker, James R. and Arthur B. Siegler, Jr., eds. *Casebook Edition of William Golding's 'Lord of the Flies': Text, Notes and Criticism.*

New York: G.P. Putnam's Sons, 1964. (No LC or ISBN is listed for this book in OCLC, CBI or the NUC.)

Biles, Jack I. and Robert O. Evans, eds. *William Golding: Some Critical Considerations*. Lexington, KY: University Press of Kentucky, 1978. LC: 77-73705. ISBN: 0-8131-1362-8.

Biles, Jack I. and William Golding. *Talk: Conversations with William Golding*. New York: Harcourt, Brace, Jovanovich, 1970. LC: 73-117570. ISBN: 0-151-87986-9.

Dick, Bernard F. "The anarchy within," and "Epilogue." *William Golding*. New York: Twayne Publishers, 1967. pp. 18-36; and 96-104. LC: 67-19351. ISBN: none listed.

Epstein, E.L. "Notes on *Lord of the Flies*; epilogue to *Lord of the Flies* by William Golding." In Lyle, Guy R., ed. *Praise from Famous Men: An Anthology of Introductions*. Metuchen, NJ: Scarecrow Press, 1977. pp. 69-74. LC: 76-55402. ISBN: 0-8108-1002-6.

Golding, William. "Fable." *The Hot Gates and Other Occasional Pieces*. New York: Harcourt, Brace & World, 1966. pp. 85-101. LC: 66-12363. ISBN: none listed.

Golding, William. "A moving target," and "Utopias and antiutopias." *In A Moving Target*. New York: Farrar, Straus & Giroux, 1982. pp. 154-170 and 171-184. LC: 82-5206. ISBN: 0-374-21573-1.

Hynes, Samuel. *William Golding*. New York: Columbia University Press, 1964. LC: 64-22638. ISBN: none listed.

Johnston, Arnold. *Of Earth and Darkness: The Novels of William Golding*. Columbia, MO: University of Missouri Press, 1980. LC: 79-3332. ISBN: 0-8262-0292-6.

Kermode, Frank. *Puzzles and Epiphanies*. London: Routledge & Kegan Paul, 1962. New York: Chilmark Press, 1962. pp. 198-218. LC: 62-15618. ISBN: none listed.

Oldsey, Bernard S. and Stanley Weintraub. *The Art of William Golding*. New York: Harcourt, Brace & World, 1965. LC: 65-23971. ISBN: none listed.

Richter, D. H. "Allegory versus fable: Golding's *Lord of the Flies*." *In Fable's End: Completeness and Closure in Rhetorical Fiction*. Chicago: University of Chicago Press, 1974. pp. 61-82. LC: 74-10344. ISBN: 0-226-71317-2.

Woodward, Kathleen M. "On aggression: William Golding's *Lord of the Flies*." In Rabkin, Eric S., Martin H. Greenberg, and Joseph D. Olander, eds. *No Place Else: Explorations in Utopian and*

Dystopian Fiction. Carbondale, IL: Southern Illinois University Press, 1983. pp. 199-224. LC: 83-4265. ISBN: 0-8093-1113-5.

Awards and Prizes

Nobel Prize for Literature, 1983. For the body of his work.

Recommended Reading Lists

Carlsen, G. Robert. *Books and the Teenage Reader, 2nd Revised Ed.* New York: Harper & Row, 1980. p. 136. LC: 78-2117. ISBN: 0-06-010626-3.

Dreyer, Sharon Spredemann. *The Bookfinder: A Guide to Children's Literature About the Needs and Problems of Youth Aged 2-15.* 3v. Circle Pines, MN: American Guidance Service, dates vary. v.1 (1977) #367. LC: 78-105919. ISBN: 0-913476-45-5.

Fiction Catalog. l0th Ed. Ed. by Juliette Yaakov and Gary L. Bogart. New York: H. W. Wilson, 1981. p. 213. LC: 81-43101. ISBN: 0-8242-0660-6.

Fiction for Youth: A Guide to Recommended Books, 2nd Ed. Ed. by Lillian L. Shapiro. New York: Neal-Schuman Publishers, 1986. p. 75. LC: 85-18857. ISBN: 0-918212-94-4.

Gilbar, Steven. *Good Books: A Book Lover's Companion.* New Haven, CT: Ticknor & Fields, 1982. p. 118. LC: 82-5554. ISBN: 0-89919-127-4.

Good Reading: A Guide for Serious Readers, 21st Ed. Ed. by J. Sherwood Weber. The Committee on College Reading. New York: R. R. Bowker Company, 1978. p. 104. LC: 78-2424. ISBN: 0-8352-1063-4.

Junior High School Catalog, 4th Ed. Ed. by Gary L. Bodart and Richard H. Isaacson. New York: H. W. Wilson, 1980. p. 411. LC: 80-53462. ISBN: 0-8242-0652-5.

The Reader's Advisor: A Layman's Guide to Literature, 13th Ed. 3v. New York: R. R. Bowker Company, 1986. v.1 pp. 385-386. LC: 57-13277. ISBN: 0-8352-2145-8.

Senior High School Library Catalog, 13th Ed. New York: H. W. Wilson, 1987. LC: 87-7377. ISBN: 0-8242-0755-6.

A Way of Love, A Way of Life:
A Young Person's Introduction to What It Means to Be Gay

By Frances Hanckel and John Cunningham

New York: Lothrop, Lee and Shepard Books, 1979. LC: 79-21813. ISBN: 0-688-41907-0.

Annotation

Written by two gay people with experience in youth service, this title is a positive informational book for young adults who are gay or think they might be gay. It covers historical, legal, sociological and biological information. Specific chapters cover how to tell whether or not you are gay, how parents and peers may react to your homosexuality, and how to locate information and assistance in your own community. A concluding chapter, "Gay Lives," features short biographical essays by twelve gay persons which demonstrate that homosexuality knows no ethnic or social boundaries.

The book provides a factual and nonjudgmental treatment of a subject that is omitted from or negatively presented in many other materials designed for young adults. It tackles the questions which young people confront in deciding on their own and other people's sexual identities, helps them discard harmful stereotypes and misinformation, and encourages them to accept themselves and others as they are.

The biographical chapter offers a sense of what it takes to succeed as a gay person in a heterosexual society, and the realization that gay people are just ordinary human beings, in many ways no different than anyone else. These concepts can go a long way in helping young adults to accept the breadth of human experience and to show tolerance for the differences between people.

While the tone of the book is reassuring, it does not gloss over the difficulties and problems of being gay, nor does it proselytize. The authors treat sexuality as one part of a total, loving relationship, and emphasize the responsibilities of both partners in any sexual activity. Information on anatomy and homosexual practices is presented factually, with clarity but without sensationalism. The authors stress the importance of making decisions and choices about your own life, establishing healthy relationships, and seeking assistance if problems or pressures occur.

Statistics indicate that at least ten percent of the total population is homosexual. This book provides a valuable resource not only for gay teens, but also for their parents, teachers, friends, counselors and families.

Examples of Recent Challenges

Challenged in Atlantic, Iowa (1982) because it is a "morally corrupting force."

Removed from two Anniston, Alabama high school libraries (1982) but later reinstated on a restrictive basis.

Challenged at the Fairbanks, Alaska North Star Borough school district libraries (1984) because schools should teach the basics, "not how to become queer dope users."

Source: The Office for Intellectual Freedom, American Library Association.

Reviews

Best Sellers. 39:353 (12/79). ISSN: 0005-0019.

Booklist. 76:229, 276 (10/1/79). ISSN: 0006-7385.

Children's Book Review Service. 8:68 (Winter Supplement 1980). ISSN: 0090-7987.

High School Journal. 63:310-311 (4/80). ISSN: 0018-1498.

Journal of Adolescent Health Care. 1:83 (9/80). ISSN: 0197-0070.

Kirkus Reviews. 47:1214 (10/15/79). ISSN: 0042-6598.

School Library Journal. 27:155 (10/80). ISSN: 0000-0035.

SIECUS Report. 8:15 (11/79). ISSN: 0091-3995.

Top of the News. 36:236 (Winter 1980). ISSN: 0040-9286.

Voice of Youth Advocates. 2:39 (2/80). ISSN: 0160-4201.

Recommended Reading Lists

Best Books for Young Adults, 1979. Young Adult Services Division. Chicago: American Library Association, 1980.

Books for the Teenage, 1986. New York Public Library.

Campbell, Patricia J. *Sex Guides: Books and Films About Sexuality for Young Adults.* New York: Garland Publishing, Inc., 1986. pp. 336, 339. LC: 85-45108. ISBN: 0-8240-8693-7.

Junior High School Catalog, 5th Ed. New York: H. W. Wilson, 1985. LC: 85-17934. ISBN: 0-8242-0720-3.

Outstanding Books for the College Bound. Young Adult Services Division. Chicago: American Library Association, 1984. p. 38. LC: 83-25714. ISBN: 0-8389-3302-5.

Senior High School Catalog, 13th Ed. New York: H. W. Wilson, 1987. pp. 71-72. LC: 87-7377. ISBN: 0-8242-0755-6.

Wilson, David E. "The open library: YA books for gay teens." *English Journal* 73:60-63 (11/84). ISSN: 0013-8274.

The Lottery

By Shirley Jackson

New York: Farrar, Straus & Giroux, 1949. LC: 49-8263. ISBN: 0-374-51681-2.
Cambridge, MA: Bentley, 1980. ISBN: 0-08376-0455-9.

Annotation

This short story, which originally appeared in the *New Yorker* in 1948, has generated an unusually strong reaction from readers. It has been widely anthologized and made into a film, and it still continues to provoke serious responses from both adult and adolescent readers and/or viewers. Jackson challenges us to examine more closely our unthinking acceptance of community traditions and values by showing us an otherwise familiar and comfortable society that has institutionalized the ritual murder of a scapegoat.

Stylistically the story is structured to contrast the ordinary routine of village life and the ominous building of tension as we begin to sense the purpose behind the gathering of stones. Still, the reader finds it difficult to grasp the horror of the conclusion and what it tells us about the "banality of evil" (in the memorable phrase of Hannah Arendt) which can infect human nature.

On the literary level, the story provides excellent examples of literary devices which lead the reader on to acceptance of the reality of Jackson's premise. Philosophically, Jackson is asking her readers to stop and consider whether the rules and standards by which we live could become as cruel and arbitrary as the annual stoning of a scapegoat in order to make the crops grow. Such uncomfortable questions may well provoke abhorrence in those who have trained themselves to value obedience and avoid any questioning of authority. But if the function of education and of libraries is to provide opportunities to develop and practice critical thinking, then few stories have more to offer than *The Lottery*.

A film of *The Lottery*, distributed by Encyclopaedia Britannica Educational Corporation, was produced in 1970, and has proved to be equally controversial as the original short story.

Examples of Recent Challenges

The film version of Jackson's short story was banned in Forest Lake, Minnesota, but reinstated by a U.S. District Court judge (1981).

Challenged in Plymouth, Michigan (1987) by a community group which made a series of complaints about films and other materials used in the school system, including *The Lottery*, on the grounds that they included obscene language, and promoted the occult, devil worship and secular humanism.

Sources: Office for Intellectual Freedom, American Library Association; and The People for the American Way.

Reviews

Booklist. 45:295 (5/1/49). ISSN: 0006-7385.

Canadian Forum. 29:94 (7/49). ISSN: 0008-3631.

Library Journal. 74:547 (4/1/49). ISSN: 0000-0027.

New Republic. 120:26 (5/9/49). ISSN: 0028-6583.

New York Herald Tribune Weekly Book Review (5/1/49).

New York Times Book Review (4/17/49). ISSN: 0028-7806.

Saturday Review of Literature. 32:19 (5/7/49). ISSN: 0361-1655.

Time. 53:105 (5/23/49). ISSN: 0040-781X.

Standard Reference Sources

Contemporary Authors, New Revision Series. Detroit: Gale Research Company, 1981. v.4. pp. 321-332. LC: 81-640179. ISSN: 0275-7176. ISBN: 0-8103-1933-0.

Supernatural Fiction Writers: Fantasy and Horror. Ed. by E. F. Bleiler. New York: Scribners, 1985. v.2 pp. 1031-1035. LC: 84-27588. ISBN: 0-684-17808-7.

Articles

Bogert, Edna.   "Censorship and *The Lottery*." *English Journal* 74:45-47 (1/85). ISSN: 0013-827.

Brown, Bill, et al. "Censoring *The Lottery*." *English Journal* 75:64-67 (2/86). ISSN: 0013-8274.

Nebeker, Helen E.   *"The Lottery*: symbolic tour de force." *American Literature* 46 (1974/1975). pp. 100-107. ISSN: 0002-9831.

Miscellaneous Discussion

Critical Survey of Short Fiction. Ed. by Frank Magill. Englewood Cliffs, NJ: Salem Press, 1981. v.2 pp. 795-796 and v.5 pp. 1168-1174. LC: 81-51697. v.2 ISBN: 0-89356-212-2; v.5 ISBN: 0-89356-215-7.

Recommended Reading Lists

Fiction Catalog, 11th Ed.   Ed. by Juliette Yaakov.   New York: H. W. Wilson, 1986. p. 318. LC: 85-32298. ISBN: 0-8242-0728-9.

Good Reading: A Guide for Serious Readers, 22nd Ed. New York: R. R. Bowker Company, 1985. p. 176. LC: 85-17459. ISBN: 0-8352-2100-8.

Senior High School Catalog, 13th Ed. New York: H. W. Wilson, 1987. p. 655. LC: 87-7377. ISBN: 0-8242-0755-6.

Your Reading: A Booklist for Junior High and Middle School Students. Ed. by Jane Christensen. Committee on the Junior High and Middle School Booklist. Urbana, IL: National Council of Teachers of English, 1983. LC: 83-17426. ISBN: 0-8141-5938-9.

Flowers for Algernon

By Daniel Keyes

New York: Harcourt, Brace and World, 1966. LC: 66-12366. ISBN: 0-15-131510-8.

Annotation

Daniel Keyes', *Flowers for Algernon*, is among the best known titles in contemporary science fiction. It appeared first as a long short story or novelette in April 1959 and won a Hugo Award from the World Science Fiction Society. It was subsequently produced as a television play and expanded into a novel in 1966 under the same title. Later it was produced as a feature film under the title of *Charly*. Thus it has achieved success in a variety of formats: as a short story, a one-act and a full-length filmplay, and a novel. Cliff Robertson won an Oscar for his portrayal of the title role in the film.

The science fiction elements in the story act more as enabling devices than as the main focus of the narrative. A scientific experiment allows the retarded Charlie Gordon gradually to become smarter and smarter, until he is a genius without equal. During this change he also becomes arrogant and overbearing in his relationships with others, although he tries to fight this change in his personality. Then the process reverses itself, and Charlie again reverts to his retarded state.

The story is told through the device of Charlie's journal. One of the brilliant aspects of Keyes' work is the gradual change we see reflected in Charlie's own words: from clumsy grammar, misspellings and awkward sentence structures, but simplicity of expression, he progresses to flawless mechanics but almost impenetrable complexity of style; all of this paralleling the change in his personality, from kind and anxious to please, to impatient and autocratic.

Most importantly, with compassion and sensitivity, the story shows the pain of being treated with condescension, the arrogance and assurance of genius, and the determination of a person who has known something wonderful and has lost it, but hangs on tightly to what he can of it.

Young readers, recognizing what Charlie has gained and lost during his transformation into genius and relapse into his retarded state, can (as Robert Carlsen, Margaret Early and others have shown) gain in conscious understanding of themselves and the people around them. They can wonder what it would be like to be as Charlie is at the beginning of the story. They can identify with and rejoice in his progress to genius, yet see how heightened intelligence and awareness might change their perceptions of other people who are not as quick. They can struggle with Charlie against the decline of his mental powers and the loss of his brilliance. And they can test their own resolve, their own capacity for affection and generosity against his.

A feature film of *Flowers for Algernon*, retitled *Charly*, was made in 1968, directed by Ralph Nelson, and distributed by Films Inc.

Examples of Recent Challenges

Banned from the Plant City, Florida (1976) and Emporium, Pennsylvania (1977) public schools because of references to sex.

Banned from the Glen Rose, Alaska High School library (1981); challenged at the Oberlin, Ohio High School (1983) because several pages of the novel detail a sexual encounter of the protagonist.

Challenged as required reading at the Glenrock, Wyoming High School (1984) because several "explicit love scenes were distasteful."

Challenged at the Charlotte-Mecklenburg, North Carolina schools (1986) as tenth grade supplemental reading because it is "pornographic."

Removed from a junior high school advanced English class in Holden, Missouri (1987) "because it uses the Lord's name in vain and contains a sexually explicit passage."

Sources: Office for Intellectual Freedom, American Library Association; and The People for the American Way.

Reviews

Best Sellers. 26:10 (4/1/66). ISSN: 0005-9730.

Booklist. 62:948 (6/1/66). ISSN: 0006-7385.

Books and Bookman. 11:34 (9/66).

English Journal. 55:619 (5/66). ISSN: 0013-8274.

Kirkus Reviews. 34:26 (1/1/66). ISSN: 0042-6598.

Library Journal. 91:965 (2/15/66). ISSN: 0000-0027.

Magazine of Fantasy and Science Fiction. 30:36 (6/66). ISSN: 0024-984X.

New Statesman. 72:136 (7/22/66). ISSN: 0028-5842.

New York Times Book Review. 115:25 (2/26/66). ISSN: 0028-7806.

Observer. (8/7/66). ISSN: 0029-7712.

Publishers Weekly. 189:91 (2/28/66). ISSN: 0000-0019.

Saturday Review. 49:33 (3/26/66). ISSN: 0361-1655.

Times Literary Supplement. (7/21/66). ISSN: 0040-7895.

Standard Reference Sources

Contemporary Authors, New Revision Series. Detroit: Gale Research Company, 1983. v.l0 pp. 262-265. LC: 81-640179. ISBN: 0-8103-1939-X. ISSN: 0275-7176.

Something About the Author. Detroit: Gale Research Company, 1985. v.37 pp. 86-88. LC: 72-27107. ISBN: 0-8103-0069-9. ISSN: 0276-816X.

Articles

Library Journal 91:728 (2/1/66). ISSN: 0000-0027.

Miscellaneous Discussion

Scoles, Robert. *Structural Fabulation*. South Bend, IN: University of Notre Dame Press, 1975. pp. 54-58. LC: 74-30167. ISBN: 0-268-00560-2; 0-268-00571-0 (pb).

Awards and Prizes

Hugo Award for Best Novelette of 1960, presented by the World Science Fiction Society.

Nebula Award for the Best Novel 1966, presented by the Science Fiction Writers of America.

Recommended Reading Lists

Books for You: A Booklist for Senior High School Students. Ed. by Robert C. Small, Jr. Urbana, IL: National Council of Teachers of English, 1982. LC: 82-8199. ISBN: 0-8141-0359-6.

Carlsen, G. Robert. *Books for the Teenage Reader, 2nd Revised Ed*. New York: Harper and Row, 1980. p. 266. LC: 78-2117. ISBN: 0-06-010626-3.

Outstanding Books for the College Bound. Young Adult Services Division. Chicago: American Library Association, 1984. LC: 83-25714. ISBN: 0-8389-3302-5.

Senior High School Library Catalog, 13th Ed. New York: H. W. Wilson, 1987. LC: 87-7377. ISBN: 0-8242-0755-6.

Cujo

By Stephen King

New York: Viking Press, 1981. LC: 81-50265. ISBN: 0-670-45193-2.

Annotation

As a study in terror, *Cujo* combines the actual menace of a mad dog with the guilty projections of the people in the novel. In the minds of the characters, the dog becomes an instrument of vengeance, punishing them for what they have done or have thought about doing.

King is particularly adroit at describing the state of mind of his victims, then using this intimacy to personalize the accidents which fate visits upon them. His characters are victims of bizarre strings of unlikely circumstances and coincidences. These convolutions of plot would have undermined the credibility of a less confident storyteller, but King seizes on their very unlikelihood to orchestrate an atmosphere of inevitable doom. There is a quasi-biblical sense of disaster as predestined or self-invoked, as gloomily satisfying to his readers as those primitive concepts of an eye for an eye, or the sins of the fathers being visited upon their children.

The preoccupations and morbid self-awareness of King's characters are appealing to teenage readers who are themselves experiencing a similar struggle of conflicting impulses and new and overpowering feelings. They too find themselves in familiar surroundings which suddenly turn alien. The genre of horror fiction, which creates worlds of deception where the rules are rigged and everybody but the protagonist seems to understand the game, has great appeal for young people who may feel caught in the same kinds of traps.

A feature film of Cujo was made in 1983; produced by Daniel H. Blatt and Robert Singer, directed by Lewis Teague, and distributed by Warner Brothers.

Examples of Recent Challenges

Challenged at the Rankin County, Mississippi school district (1984) because it is "profane and sexually objectionable."

Removed from the shelves of the Bradford, New York school library (1985) "because it was a bunch of garbage."

Rejected for purchase by the Hayward, California school trustees (1985) because of the "rough language" and "explicit sex scenes."

The Washington County, Alabama Board of Education (1985) voted unanimously to ban the novel from all county school libraries because the book contains "unacceptable language" and is "pornographic."

Restricted to senior high school students in the Lincoln, Nebraska junior-senior high school media center (1987) because of "profanity, sexual scenes and violence."

Sources: Office for Intellectual Freedom, American Library Association; and The People for the American Way.

Reviews

Booklist. 77:1213 (5/15/81). ISSN: 0006-7385.

Library Journal. 106:1443 (7/81). ISSN: 0363-0277.

Newsweek. 98:64 (8/31/81). ISSN: 0028-9604.

Publishers Weekly. 220:80 (7/17/81). ISSN: 0000-0019.

Saturday Review. 8:59 (9/81). ISSN: 0091-620X.

School Library Journal. 28:162 (10/81). ISSN: 0000-0035.

Voice of Youth Advocates. 4:34 (10/81). ISSN: 0160-4201.

Washington Post Book World. (8/23/81). ISSN: 0006-7369.

Standard Reference Sources

Contemporary Authors, New Revision Series. Detroit: Gale Research Company, 1981.   v.1 pp. 333-336.   LC: 62-52046. ISBN: 0-8103-1930-6.

Contemporary Literary Criticism. Detroit: Gale Research Company, 1983. v.26 pp. 234-244. LC: 76-38938. ISBN: 0-8103-4400-9. v.37 pp. 197-208. LC: 76-38938. ISBN: 0-8103-4411-4.

Penguin Encyclopedia of Horror and the Supernatural. Ed. by Jack Sullivan. New York: Viking Press, 1986. pp. 243-246. LC: 85-40558. ISBN: 0-670-80902-0.

Who's Who in Horror and Fantasy Fiction. Ed. by Mike Ashley. New York: Taplinger Press, 1978. p. 107. LC: 77-4608. ISBN: 0-8008-8278-4.

Articles

Bandler, M. J.   "The king of the macabre at home." *Parent's Magazine* 57:68-72 (1/82). ISSN: 0161-4193.

Cohen, Barney.   "The shockmeisters." *Esquire* 102:231-232 (11/84). ISSN: 0194-9535.

Gray, P. "Master of postliterate prose." *Time* 120:87 (8/30/82). ISSN: 0040-781X.

Janeczko, Paul.   "An interview with Stephen King." *English Journal* 69:9-10 (2/80). ISSN: 0013-8274.

Kendrick, Walter. "Stephen King gets eminent." *Village Voice* 26:45 (4/29-5/5/81). ISSN: 0042-6180.

Leerhsen, C. "The titans of terror." *Newsweek* 104:61-62 (12/24/84). ISSN: 0028-9604.

McGrath, Id C. *New Yorker* 62:24-26 (12/29/86). ISSN: 0028-792X.

Phippen, Sanford. "Stephen King's appeal to youth." *Maine Life* 1:44 (12/80). ISSN: 0025-0678.

Slung, Michele. "A master of the macabre." *New Republic* 184:38-39 (2/21/81). ISSN: 0028-6583.

Miscellaneous Discussion

Bare Bones: Conversations on Terror with Stephen King. Ed. by Tim Underwood and Chuck Miller. New York: McGraw-Hill, 1988. LC: 87-31078. ISBN: 0-07-065759-9.

Bosky, Bernadette Lynn. "The mind's a monkey: character and psychology in Stephen King's recent fiction." In *Kingdom of Fear: The World of Stephen King.* Ed. by Tim Underwood and Chuck Miller. New York: New American Library, 1986. pp. 209-237. LC: 86-12868. ISBN: 0-452-25875-8.

Collings, Michael R. *The Many Facets of Stephen King.* Mercer Island, WA: Starmont House, 1985. pp. 44-53. LC: 85-12598. ISBN: 0-930261-15-1.

Discovering Stephen King. Ed. by Darrell Schweitzer. Mercer Island, WA: Starmont House, 1985. LC: 85-2821. ISBN: 0-930261-07-0.

Fear Itself: The Horror Fiction of Stephen King. Ed. by Tim Underwood and Chuck Miller. San Francisco, CA and Columbia, PA: Underwood-Miller, 1982. LC: 83-24990. ISBN: 0-934438-59-5.

Hatlen, Burton. "The mad dog and Maine." *Shadowings: The Reader's Guide to Horror Fiction, 1981-82.* Ed. by Douglas E. Winter. Mercer Island, WA: Starmont House, 1983. LC: 83-21326. ISBN: 0-916732-86-X.

King, Stephen. *Stephen King's Danse Macabre.* New York: Everest House, 1981. LC: 79-28056. ISBN: 0-89696-076-5.

Patrouch, Joseph F., Jr. "Stephen King in context." In *Patterns of the Fantastic I: Academic Programming at Chicon IV.* Ed. by Donald M. Hassler. Mercer Island, WA: Starmont House, 1983. pp. 5-10. LC: 83-587. ISBN: O-916732-63-0.

Winter, Douglas E. *Stephen King: The Art of Darkness*, Revised Ed. New York: New American Library, 1986. pp. 107-116. LC: 84-1167. ISBN: 0-451-14612-3.

Recommended Reading Lists

Books for the Teen Age, 1986. Office of Young Adult Services, New York Public Library.

Books for You: A Booklist for Senior High Students. Ed. by Donald R. Gallo. Committee on the Senior High School Booklist. Urbana, IL: National Council of Teachers of English, 1985. p. 169. LC: 85-21666. ISBN: 0-8141-0363-4.

Fiction Catalog, 11th Ed. Ed. by Juliette Yaakov. New York: H. W. Wilson, 1986. p. 646. LC: 85-32298. ISBN: 0-8242-0728-9.

Kies, Cosette. *Supernatural Fiction for Teens: 500 Good Paperbacks to Read for Wonderment, Fear, and Fun.* Littleton, CO: Libraries Unlimited, 1987. pp. 42-43. LC: 87-3228. ISBN: 0-87287-602-0.

Rosenberg, Betty. *Genreflections: A Guide to Reading Interests in Genre Fiction*, 2nd Ed. Littleton, CO: Libraries Unlimited, 1986. pp. 251-252. LC: 86-21489. ISBN: 0-87287-530-X.

The Last Mission

By Harry Mazer

New York: Delacorte Press, 1979. LC: 79-50674. ISBN: 0-440-05774-4.

Annotation

Fifteen-year-old Jack Raab, a Jewish boy from Brooklyn, New York, lies about his age so that he can join the army and fight for glory and the defeat of Hitler, during World War II.   On its twenty-fifth mission his bomber is shot down and Jack, the only survivor of the crash, is captured by the Germans and sent to a prisoner-of-war camp.

Challenges to this vividly realized portrait of one boy's wartime experiences usually focus on the vulgar language of the soldiers, but individuals may also object to Jack's realization that "War is stupid.   War is one stupid thing after another," as undermining patriotism and respect for authority.

Stories which present wartime experiences as a "rite of passage" have been a staple of literature since the time of Homer. Jack grows up through his fight for survival in the midst of war. One way in which we see him change is in his gradual adoption of swearing. The language metaphorically expresses Jack's loss of innocence and the death of his idealistic fantasies in the face of his actual experiences. Seldom has a young adult author used "bad" language with greater artistic control and effect.

Moreover, the author has stated that this use of language was not only deliberate but also based on his own experiences as a soldier in World War II.   He revealed that soldiers returning home from that war had worried about how they would be able to adjust to talking like civilians again. Many men who have been in combat might agree that the profanity of war cannot be articulated without resorting to profane language. *The Last Mission* is one of the most authentic and convincing stories of war accessible to teens.   Certainly if American society considers eighteen-year-olds ready to experience the reality of combat in wartime, then younger teens should be allowed to read about the experience of combat.

Examples of Recent Challenges

Challenged at the Pequannock Valley Middle School in Pompton Plains, New Jersey (1984) because of its "language."

Moved from the Alexander Middle School library to the Nekoosa, Wisconsin High School library (1986) because of "profanity" in the book.

Source: The Office for Intellectual Freedom, American Library Association.

Reviews

Best Sellers. 39:466 (3/80). ISSN: 0005-9625.

Childhood Education. 56:305 (4/80). ISSN: 0009-4056.

Children's Book Review Service. 8:18 (10/79). ISSN: 0090-7987.

English Journal. 69:93-94 (5/80). ISSN: 0013-8274.

Hornbook. 56:63 (2/80). ISSN: 0018-5078.

Journal of Reading. 24:85 (10/80). ISSN: 0022-4103.

Kirkus Reviews. 48:10 (1/1/80). ISSN: 0042-6598.

Kliatt. 15:11 (Spring 1981). ISSN: 0199-2376.

New York Times Book Review. (12/2/79). ISSN: 0028-7806.

Publishers Weekly. 216:70 (12/10/79). ISSN: 0000-0019.

School Library Journal. 26:91 (11/79). ISSN: 0000-0035.

Voice of Youth Advocates. 3:35 (4/80). ISSN: 0160-4201.

Wilson Library Bulletin. 54:139 (10/79). ISSN: 0043-5651.

Standard Reference Sources

Contemporary Authors. Detroit: Gale Research Company, 1981. v.97-100 pp. 355-358. LC: 62-52046. ISBN: 0-8103-0057-5.

Something About the Author. Detroit: Gale Research Company, 1983. v.31 pp. 126-131. LC: 72-27107. ISBN: 0-8103-0057-5. ISSN: 0276-816X.

Awards and Prizes

New York Times Best Books of the Year, 1979.

Recommended Reading Lists

Bernstein, Joan E. *Books to Help Children Cope with Separation and Loss*, 2nd Ed. New York: R. R. Bowker, 1983. pp. 296-97. LC: 83-7058. ISBN: 0-835-21484-2.

Best Books for Young Adults, 1979. Young Adult Services Division. Chicago: American Library Association, 1980.

Books for the Teen Age, 1980. New York Public Library.

Books for You: A Booklist for Senior High Students. Ed. by Donald R. Gallo. Committee on the Senior High School Booklist. Urbana, IL: National Council of Teachers of English, 1985. p. 323. LC: 85-21666. ISBN: 0-8141-0363-4.

Dreyer, Sharon Spredemann. *The Bookfinder.* Circle Pines, MN; American Guidance Service, 1985. v.3 p. 235. LC: 78-105919. ISBN: 0-913476-48-X.

High Interest, Easy Reading. Committee to Revise High Interest, Easy Reading. Urbana, IL: National Council of Teachers of English, 1984. p. 4. LC: 83-25107. ISBN: 0-8141-12095-4.

Junior High School Library Catalog, 5th Ed. New York: H. W. Wilson, 1985. LC: 85-17934. ISBN: 0-8242-0720-3.

Your Reading: A Booklist for Junior High and Middle School Students. Ed. by Jane Christensen. Committee on the Junior High and Middle School Booklist. Urbana, IL: National Council of Teachers of English, 1983. p. 260. LC: 83-17426. ISBN: 0-8141-5938-9.

The Great Gilly Hopkins

By Katherine Paterson

New York: Crowell Junior Books, 1978. LC: 77-2705. ISBN 0-690-03837-2.

Annotation

The Great Gilly Hopkins was published between Katherine Paterson's two Newbery Award-winning novels, *Bridge to Terabithia* and *Jacob, Have I Loved*. Although it won the National Book Award for children's fiction and was a Newbery Honor Book, it has not received the same attention as Paterson's other award-winning, realistic novels for young readers. It is a favorite of Paterson's many fans, however, because of its strong and memorable characterizations.

Readers vividly remember fat and careless Maime Trotter, whose love and determination salvage Gilly from the scrap heap of her neglected existence. They want to protect frail William Ernest and give him the affection he craves and so generously rewards. Mr. Randolph, the elderly, blind black man who hangs on to his independence but shares dinner with Maime and her household every night, is a fully realized character and a role model of human dignity and self-respect for young readers.

But most of all it is Gilly herself who gives the novel its spice and poignancy. A many-times foster child, shuttled about like unclaimed luggage from home to home, Gilly has become tough and profane. As a result of neglect and abuse life for Gilly has been mostly a series of hard knocks, and she has learned to hit first and hit hard to survive. She will fight back even when, as with Maime, there is no apparent reason to fight, but even a good situation makes Gilly angry. The certainty of eventual loss, always at the back of Gilly's mind, makes her anger and resentment plausible, her actions logical.

Fiction (and not just fiction for young readers) has given us few such characters who have the spunk and the fierce determination to take on life and win on any terms. Becky Sharp in Thackeray's *Vanity Fair*, Tom Jones in Fielding's novel of the same name, and Mark Twain's Huckleberry Finn are some other examples. The hero who is also a rogue, living by his wits and surmounting the obstacles placed in his path by a society which has cast him off, is part of the picaresque tradition dating back to Cervantes' *Don Quixote* and even beyond.

Gilly Hopkins is a disturbing and uncomfortable book because it tries to portray the plight of the foster child honestly. Katherine Paterson has admitted that the novel grew out of her own not very successful attempt to serve as a foster parent. These children are unwanted and they know themselves to be unwanted. Some are so desperate for love that they become easy prey for anyone who will offer them attention on any terms. Others, like Gilly, have hardened themselves so as not to feel the pain and disappointment of constant rejection.   They will take whatever they can get and run.

The theme of this novel is important.   The fact that it treats a serious subject in profound terms and makes no sentimental compromises is important.   The fact that it is flawlessly written is also important. But the characters are its glory and greatness. Natalie Babbitt, in her review of *The Great Gilly Hopkins*, said: "Its characters linger long in the reader's thoughts after it is finished.   What Paterson has done is to combine a beautiful fairness with her affection for her creations, which makes them solidly three-dimensional."

Paterson's characters are not only unforgettable, but are also real. Young readers who have met them on their own terms in the pages of the book will be better equipped to understand the people like them which they meet every day in the world outside of fiction.

Examples of Recent Challenges

Challenged at the Lowell Elementary School in Salina, Kansas (1983) because the book used the words "God," "damn" and "hell" offensively.

Challenged at the Orchard Lake Elementary School library in Burnsville, Minnesota (1985) because "the book took the Lord's name in vain," and had "over forty instances of profanity."

Source: The Office for Intellectual Freedom, American Library Association.

Reviews

Booklist. 74:1194 (3/17/78). ISSN: 0006-7385.

Center for Children's Books Bulletin. 31:146-147 (5/78). ISSN: 0008-9036.

Catholic Library World. 50:180 (11/78). ISSN: 0008-820X.

Childhood Education. 55:224 (2/79). ISSN: 0009-4056.

Children's Book Review Service. 6:89 (4/74). ISSN: 0090-7987.

Commonweal. 105:732 (11/10/78); 107:113 (2/29/80). ISSN: 0010-3330.

English Journal. 69:87 (9/80). ISSN: 0013-8274.

Hornbook. 54:279 (6/78). ISSN: 0018-5078.

Junior Book Shelf. 43:283 (10/79). ISSN: 0022-6505.

Kirkus Review. 46:178 (2/15/78). ISSN: 0042-6598.

Language Arts. 56:52 (1/79). ISSN: 0013-5968.

New York Times Book Review. 83:54 (4/30/78). ISSN: 0028-7806.

Observer. (8/5/79). ISSN: 0029-7712.

Reading Teacher. 32:736 (3/79). ISSN: 0034-0561.

School Librarian. 27:383 (12/79). ISSN: 0036-6595.

School Library Journal. 24:87 (4/78). ISSN: 0000-0035.

Teacher 96:108 (5/79). ISSN: 0148-6578.

Times Literary Supplement. (12/14/79). ISSN: 0307-6614.

Washington Post Book World. (12/3/78); (2/24/80). ISSN: 0006-7369.

Standard Reference Sources

Children's Literature Review. Detroit: Gale Research Company, 1984. v.7 pp. 224-238. LC: 75-34953. ISBN: 0-8103-0344-2. ISSN: 0362-4145.

Contemporary Authors, Revised Edition. Detroit: Gale Research Company, 1977. v.21-24 p. 662. LC: 62-52046. ISBN: 0-8103-033-8.

Contemporary Literary Criticism. Detroit: Gale Research Company, 1980. v.12 pp. 484-487. LC: 76-38938. ISBN: 0-8103-0122-9. 1984. v.30 pp. 282-290. ISBN: 0-8103-4401-1.

Smedman, M. Sarah. "Katherine Paterson." *Dictionary of Literary Biography: American Writers for Children Since 1960: Fiction.* Detroit: Gale Research Company, 1986. v.52 pp. 286-314. LC: 83-14199. ISBN: 0-8103-1730-3.

Something About the Author. Detroit: Gale Research Company, 1978. v.13. pp. 176-178. LC: 72-27107. ISBN: 0-8103-0069-0. ISSN: 0276-816X.

Articles

Babbitt, Natalie. "A home for nobody's child." *Washington Post Book World* (5/14/78). ISSN: 0006-736.

Bell, Anthea. "A case of commitment." *Signal* 38:73-81 (5/82). ISSN: 0037-4954.

Solt, Marilyn. "*The Great Gilly Hopkins*." In *Newbery and Caldecott Medal and Honor Books: An Annotated Bibliography.* Ed. by Linda K. Peterson and Marilyn Solt. Boston: G.K. Hall, 1982. pp. 216-218. LC: 82-2880. ISBN: 0-8161-8448-4.

Awards and Prizes

Christopher Book Award: Juvenile, 1979
Garden State Children's Book Award, 1981
Georgia Children's Book Award, 1981
Iowa Children's Choice Award, 1981
Massachusetts Children's Book Award, 1981
National Book Award: Children's Literature, 1979

Newbery Honor Book, 1979
William Allen White Award, 1981

**Recommended
Reading Lists**

Adventuring with Books: A Booklist for Pre-K--Grade 6. Ed. by Mary Lou White. Committee on the Elementary School Booklist. Urbana, IL: National Council of Teachers of English, 1981. LC: 81-11179. ISBN: 0-8141-0075-9.

Children's Catalog, 15th Ed. New York: H. W. Wilson, 1986. LC: 86-15751. ISBN: 0-8242-0743-2.

Dreyer, Sharon Spredemann. *The Bookfinder: A Guide to Children's Literature About the Needs and Problems of Youth Aged 2-15.* 3v. Circle Pines, MN: American Guidance Service, dates vary. v.2 (1981) #494. LC: 78-105919. ISBN: 0-913476-46-3.

Helbig, Alethea K. and Agnes Regan Perkins. *Dictionary of American Children's Fiction, 1960-1984: Recent Books of Recognized Merit.* New York: Greenwood Press, 1986. pp. 255-256. LC: 85-24778. ISBN: 0-313-25233-5.

Junior High School Library Catalog, 5th Ed. New York: H. W. Wilson, 1985. LC: 85-17934. ISBN: 0-8242-0720-3.

Larrick, Nancy. "Books they like." In *A Parent's Guide to Children's Reading, 5th Ed.* Philadelphia: Westminster Press, 1982. pp. 69, 76, 78, 210. LC: 82-24702. ISBN: 0-664-32705-2.

New Paperbacks for Young Adults: A Thematic Guide, 2nd Ed. Ed. by Fay Blostein. Toronto: Ontario Library Association, 1981. ISBN: 0-88969-024-3.

Notable Children's Books, 1978. Association for Library Service to Children. Chicago: American Library Association, 1978.

Spirt, Diana L. *Introducing More Books; A Guide for the Middle Grades.* New York: R. R. Bowker, 1978. pp. 183-186. LC: 78-13490. ISBN: 0-8352-0988-1.

Your Reading: A Booklist for Junior High and Middle School Students. Ed. by Jane Christensen. Committee on the Junior High and Middle School Booklist. Urbana, IL: National Council of Teachers of English, 1983. LC: 83-17426. ISBN: 0-8141-5938-9.

A Day No Pigs Would Die

By Robert Newton Peck

New York: Knopf, 1973. LC: 72-259. ISBN: 0-394-48235-2.

Annotation

This book is a plain-spoken work about people poor in worldly possessions but rich in understanding of and appreciation for the basic and necessary acts of life. Robert Newton Peck's *A Day No Pigs Would Die* belongs to that almost defunct school of American literature called regionalism. Peck has provided his readers with a window onto a landscape that has largely disappeared from the contemporary literary scene---those isolated and impoverished but proud pockets of rural America which constituted the heart and soul of our literary self-consciousness up until forty years ago.

A Day No Pigs Would Die, through the intensity of its first-person narration and the pungency of its colloquial language, immerses its readers in the earthy and unsparing struggle of working a living out of the land. It is a conservative book, honoring the virtues and values of a sterner, stricter creed. Yet it also shows that strong convictions and intolerance of others need not go hand-in-hand. It shows how people of good will can agree to differ and still live in harmony. It argues that compassion and forgiveness are just as important as justice. And it demonstrates how growth and maturity can result not only from some great and wrenching change, but from the accumulation of small but significant choices made in the ordinary course of everyday life.

Those passages which frankly describe men and beasts behaving according to their natural instincts are essential to Peck's avowed intention of providing his readers with an honest and unvarnished account of life lived close to nature. In this regard, *A Day No Pigs Would Die* is an excellent example of literary realism, and an opportunity to examine the real life experience which formed those values we call traditional to America.

Best of all, this book is a tribute, honest, unsparing and loving, written by a son to the father he honors but never idolizes.

Examples of Recent Challenges

Challenged in the Jefferson County, Colorado school libraries (1988) because "it is bigoted against Baptists and women and depicts violence, hatred, animal cruelty, and murder." Challenged in the Adams County (Colorado) School District 50 for graphic language and derogatory references to Baptists.

Reviews

Atlantic Monthly. 231:114 (4/73) ISSN: 0004-6795.

Christian Science Monitor. 65:11 (1/17/73).

Hornbook. 49:472 (10/73). ISSN: 0018-5078.

Library Journal. 97:3728 (11/15/72). 98:1022 (3/15/73). ISSN: 0363-0277.

New York Times Book Review. (5/13/73). ISSN: 0028-7806.

Newsweek. 81:96 (3/12/73). ISSN: 0028-9604.

Times Literary Supplement. (8/17/73). ISSN: 0040-7895.

Standard Reference Sources

Contemporary Authors. Ed. by Frances Carol Locher. Detroit: Gale Research Company, 1979. v.81-84 pp. 442-443. LC: 62-52046. ISBN: 0-8103-0046-X.

Something About the Author. Ed. by Anne Commire. Detroit: Gale Research Company, 1980. v.21 pp. 113-114. LC: 72-27107. ISBN: 0-8103-0093-1.

Awards and Prizes

Colorado Children's Book Award 1977 (Colorado Library Association).
Media and Methods Maxi Award for best paperback 1975 (*Media and Methods* Magazine).

Recommended Reading Lists

Bookfinder: A Guide to Children's Literature About the Needs and Problems of Youth Aged 12-15.   Ed. by Sharon Spredemann Dreyer. Circle Pines, MN: American Guidance Service, Inc., 1977. v.1 #697. LC: 78-105919. ISBN: 0-913476-45-5.

Carlsen, G. Robert. *Books and the Teenage Reader, 2nd Revised Ed.* New York: Harper and Row, 1980. p. 80. LC: 78-2117. ISBN: 0-06-010626-3.

Fiction Catalog, 11th Ed. New York. H. W. Wilson, 1986. p. 475. LC: 85-32298. ISBN: 0-8242-0728-9.

Fiction for Youth: A Guide to Recommended Books, 2nd Ed. Ed. by Lillian L. Shapiro. New York: Neal-Schuman Publishers, Inc., 1986. p. 151. LC: 85-18857. ISBN: 0-918212-94-4.

Gillespie, John T. *More Junior Plots: A Guide for Teachers and Librarians.* New York: R. R. Bowker Company, 1977. pp. 16-19. LC: 77-8786. ISBN: 0-8352-1002-2.

Helbig, Alethea K. and Agnes Regan Perkins. *Dictionary of American Children's Fiction, 1960-1984: Recent Books of Recognized Merit.* New York: Greenwood Press, 1986. pp. 149-150. LC: 85-24778. ISBN: 0-313-25233-5.

Junior High School Library Catalog, 4th Ed. New York: H. W. Wilson, 1980. p. 441. LC: 80-53462. ISBN: 0-8242-0652-5.

Senior High School Catalog, 13th Ed. New York: H. W. Wilson, 1987. p. 629. LC: 87-7377. lSBN: 0-8242-0755-6.

The Catcher in the Rye

By J. D. (Jerome David) Salinger

Boston: Little, Brown & Co., 1951. LC: 51:4713. ISBN: 0-316-76953-3.

Annotation

It is interesting and ironic that Salinger's *The Catcher in the Rye* is considered both a major work, even a benchmark of postwar American literature, and the progenitor or prototype of the contemporary "young adult problem" novel. Its impact on the literary world of the 1950s and 1960s was nothing short of phenomenal. Salinger was hailed as one of the first of those angry voices which railed against the smug self-satisfaction of the postwar boom years, when middleclass America perceived itself as the navel of the world.

The novel was controversial from the start, and remains so today. The cause of the complaints has never changed: the book is condemned for the "bad grammar" and "vulgar language" of its protagonist and narrator, Holden Caulfield, a seventeen-year-old prep school dropout, and for Holden's preoccupation (some would say obsession) with death and sex.

But these aspects of the book are not cynical attempts to titillate or shock, but deliberate patterns which reveal the purpose or theme of the novel. And Salinger's theme is neither new nor revolutionary; he deals with the difficulty of growing up, or reaching maturity and achieving a sense of self-worth in a cold and uncaring world preoccupied with the appearances rather than the realities of life. Holden's story is one more example of the literary tradition of the "rite of passage" story---the lonely and arduous journey from childhood innocence to adult experience and responsibility.

We meet Holden at just that uncomfortable point of exposure when he is hanging undecided, unprotected, without defenses and so vulnerable, halfway between childhood and adulthood. The difficulty for Holden is that he sees children as dealing directly and clearly with the realities of life, while adults and those who emulate adults are content to deal with appearances. His dilemma is how he can preserve the clear eyes and honesty of childhood as he moves inexorably toward the experiences of adulthood.

This way of perceiving the "rite of passage" is nothing new, but Salinger breaks with traditional literary format by structuring his story, not linearly, but in a circle or spiral. Holden advances not by moving forward from one experience to the next, but by going round and round, examining and reinventing his experiences. Such subjectivity in narrative structure and purpose is one of the hallmarks of modern literary technique.

Salinger chooses his words quite deliberately to distinguish between the formal, genteel and empty appearances of the "phony" adult world, and the confusing, conflicting impulses of Holden's reality. Holden's language is honest in expressing this confusion and conflict. If we define vulgarity as that which makes people uncomfortable with themselves, then Holden's so-called vulgar language reveals just how uncomfortable we are with his honesty, how unprepared we are to deal with his pain.

Examples Recent Challenges

Since its publication, this title has been a favorite target of censors. Recent examples include its removal from the Issaquah, Washington optional high school reading list (1978). Removed from the required reading list in Middleville, Michigan (1979).

Removed from the Jackson-Milton school libraries in North Jackson, Ohio (1980). Removed from two Anniston, Alabama high school libraries (1982), but later reinstated on a restrictive basis.

Removed from the school libraries in Morris, Manitoba (1982) along with two other books because they violated the committee's guidelines covering "excess vulgar language, sexual scenes, things concerning moral issues, excessive violence, and anything dealing with the occult."

Challenged at the Libby, Montana High School (1983) due to the "book's contents." Banned from English classes at the Freeport High School in De Funiak Springs, Florida (1985) because it is "unacceptable" and "obscene."

Removed from the required reading list of a Medicine Bow, Wyoming Senior High School English class (1986) because of sexual references and profanity in the book.

Removed from the optional reading list for eleventh and twelfth grade English classes at the Lamar, Missouri Senior High School after a school board member complained about the book's "foul language, use of the Lord's name in vain, and sexual overtones." The school board retained the book in the school library.

Sources: The Office for Intellectual Freedom, American Library Association; and The People for the American Way.

Reviews

Atlantic. 188:82 (8/51). ISSN: 0004-6795.

Booklist. 47:401 (7/15/51). ISSN: 0006-7385.

Catholic World. 174:154 (11/51). ISSN: 0008-848X.

Chicago Tribune. (7/15/51).

Christian Science Monitor. 43:7 (7/19/51).

Kirkus Reviews. 19:247 (5/15/51). ISSN: 0042-6598.

Library Journal. 76:1125 (7/51). ISSN: 0363-0277.

Nation. 173:176 (9/1/51). ISSN: 0027-8378.

New Republic. 125:20 (7/16/51). ISSN: 0028-6583.

New York Herald Tribune Book Review. (7/15/51).

New York Times. (7/15/51).

New Yorker. 27:71 (8/11/51). ISSN: 0028-792X.

Newsweek. 38:89 (7/16/51). ISSN: 0028-9604.

San Francisco Chronicle. (7/15/51).

Saturday Review. 34:12 (7/14/51). ISSN: 0036-4983.

Time. 58:96 (7/16/51). ISSN: 0040-781X.

Times Literary Supplement. (9/7/51). ISSN: 0040-7895.

Standard Reference Sources

American Writers: A Collection of Literary Biographies, 4v. Ed. by Leonard Unger. New York: Scribner's, 1974. v.3 pp. 551-574. LC: 73-1759. ISBN: 0-684-13675-9.

Contemporary Authors, 1st Revision Series. Detroit: Gale Research Company, 1969. v.5-8 pp. 997-999. LC: 62-52046. ISBN: 0-8103-0001-X.

Contemporary Literary Criticism. Editors vary. Detroit: Gale Research Company, dates vary.
v.1   pp. 295-300   (1973) LC: 76-38938 ISBN: 0-8103-0100-8
v.3   pp. 444-446   (1975) LC: 76-38938 ISBN: 0-8103-0104-0
v.8   pp. 463-465   (1978) LC: 76-38938 ISBN: 0-8103-0114-8
v.12 pp. 496-521   (1980) LC: 76-38938 ISBN: 0-8103-0122-9

Contemporary Novelists, 4th Ed. Ed. by D. L. Kirkpatrick. New York: St. Martin's Press, 1986. pp. 733-735. LC: 86-13904. ISBN: 0-312-16731-8.

Dictionary of Literary Biography; Volume 2: American Novelists Since World War II. Ed. by Jeffrey Helterman and Richard Layman. Detroit: Gale Research Company, 1978. pp. 434-444. LC: 77-82804. ISBN: 0-8103-0914-9.

Encyclopedia of World Literature in the 20th Century, Revised Ed. 4v. Ed. by Leonard S. Klein. New York: Frederick Ungar, 1984. v. 4 pp. 135-137. LC: 81-3357. ISBN: 0-8044-3138-8.

Reference Guide to American Literature, 2nd Ed. Ed. by D. L. Kirkpatrick. Chicago: St. James Press, 1987. pp. 477-478, 620-621. LC: none listed. ISBN: 0-912289-61-9.

Articles

Barr, Donald. "Should Holden Caulfield read these books?" *New York Times Book Review* 91:1+50-51 (5/4/86). ISSN: 0028-7806.

Bryan, James E. "The psychological structure of *The Catcher in the Rye*." *PMLA* 89:1064-1074 (10/74). ISSN: 0030-8129.

Coles, Robert. "Reconsideration: J. D. Salinger." *New Republic* 168:30-32 (4/28/73). ISSN: 0028-6583.

Costello, Donald P. "The language of *The Catcher in the Rye*." *American Speech* 34:172-181 (10/59). ISSN: 0003-1283.

De Luca, Geraldine. "Unself-conscious voices; larger contexts for adolescents." *The Lion and the Unicorn* 2:89-108 (Fall/78).   ISSN: 0147-2593.

Glasser, William.   *The Catcher in the Rye*." *Michigan Quarterly Review* 15:432-455 (Fall/76). ISSN: 0026-2420.

Kaplan, Charles. "Holden and Huck: the odyssey of youth." *College English* 28:76-80 (11/56). ISSN: 0010-0994.

Kazin, Alfred. "J. D. Salinger: everybody's favorite." *Atlantic* 208:27-31 (8/61). ISSN: 0004-6795.

Moss, A. "Catcher comes of age." *Esquire* 96:56-58+ (12/81). ISSN: 0194-9835.

Ohmann, Carol and Richard Ohmann. "Reviews, critics, and *The Catcher in the Rye*." *Critical Inquiry* 3:15-38 (Autumn/76). ISSN: 0093-1896.

Pinsker, S. "*The Catcher in the Rye* and all: is the age of formative books over?" *Georgia Review* 40:953-967 (Winter/86). ISSN: 0016-8386.

Slabey, Robert M. "*The Catcher in the Rye*: Christian theme and symbol." *College Language Association Journal* 6:170-183 (3/63). ISSN: 0007-8549.

Special Number: Salinger. *Wisconsin Studies in Contemporary Literature* 4:1-160 (Winter/63).   ISSN: 0010-7484.

Strauch, Carl F. "Kings in the back row: meaning through structure---a reading of Salinger's *The Catcher in the Rye*." *Wisconsin Studies in Contemporary Literature* 2:5-30 (Winter/61). ISSN: 0010-7484.

Teachout, T. "Salinger then and now." *Commentary* 84:61-64 (9/87). ISSN: 0010-2601.

Miscellaneous Discussion

Baumbach, Jonathan. "The saint as a young man: *The Catcher in the Rye* by J. D. Salinger." In *The Landscape of Nightmare; Studies in the Contemporary American Novel.* New York: New York University Press, 1965. pp. 57-67. LC: 65-11761. ISBN: 0-8147-0031-4.

Dessner, L. J. "The Salinger story; or, have it your way." *In Seasoned Authors for a New Season: The Search for Standards in Popular Writing.* 2v. Ed. by Louis Filler. Bowling Green, OH: Bowling Green University Popular Press, 1980. v.2 pp. 91-97. LC: 79-90128. ISBN: 0-87972-143-X.

French, Warren. *J. D. Salinger, 2nd Revised Ed.* Boston: G.K. Hall (Twayne's U.S. Author Series), 1976. LC: 79-910. ISBN: 0-8057-7163-8.

Gwynn, Frederick L. and Joseph Blotner. *The Fiction of J. D. Salinger.* Pittsburgh, PA: University of Pittsburgh Press, 1958. LC: 58-14389. ISBN: 0-8229-5019-7.

Hamilton, Ian. *J. D. Salinger: A Writing Life.* London: Heinemann, 1986; New York: Random House, 1986. LC: 85-25591. ISBN: 0-394-53468-9.

Harper, Howard M., Jr. "J. D. Salinger---through the glasses darkly." In *Desperate Faith; A Study of Bellow, Salinger, Mailer, Baldwin and Updike.* Chapel Hill, NC: University of North Carolina Press, 1967. pp. 65-95. LC: 67-17034. ISBN: 0-8078-4021-1.

Hassan, Ihab H. "J. D. Salinger: the quixotic gesture." In *Radical Innocence; Studies in the Contemporary American Novel.* Princeton, NJ: Princeton University Press, 1961. pp. 259-289. LC: 61-7416. ISBN: 0-691-06107-6.

Howe, Irving. "The Salinger cult." In *Celebrations and Attacks; 30 Years of Literary and Cultural Commentary.* New York: Horizon Press, 1979. pp. 93-96. LC: 78-51814. ISBN: 0-8180-1176-9.

J. D. Salinger. Ed. by Harold Bloom. New York: Chelsea House, 1987. LC: 86-29941. ISBN: 0-87754-716-5.

Lundquist, James. *J. D. Salinger.* New York: Frederick Ungar, 1978. LC: 78-4301. ISBN: 0-8044-2560-4.

Rees, R. "The Salinger situation." In *Contemporary American Novelists.* Ed. by Harry Thornton Moore. Carbondale, IL: Southern Illinois University Press, 1964. pp. 95-105. LC: 64-20254. ISBN: 0-8093-0141-5.

Riggan, William. "The naif." In *Picaros, Madmen, Naifs, and Clowns: The Unreliable First-Person Narrator*. Norman, OK: University of Oklahoma Press, 1981. pp. 144-170. LC: 81-2791. ISBN: 0-8061-1714-1.

Salinger; A Critical and Personal Portrait. Ed. by Henry A. Grunwald. New York: Harper and Row, 1962. LC: 62-11222. ISBN: none listed.

Salinger's Catcher in the Rye: Clamor Vs. Criticism. Ed. by Harold P. Simonson and Philip E. Hager. Boston: D. C. Heath & Company, 1963. LC: 64-1173. ISBN: none listed.

Studies in J. D. Salinger: Reviews, Essays, and Critiques of The Catcher in the Rye and Other Fiction. Ed. by Marvin Laser and Norman Freeman. New York: Odyssey Press, 1963. LC: 63-14023. ISBN: none listed.

Weinberg, Helen. "J. D. Salinger's Holden and Seymour and the spiritual activist hero." In *The New Novel in America: The Kafkan Mode in Contemporary Fiction*. Ithaca, NY: Cornell University Press, 1970. pp. 141-164. LC: 70-87011. ISBN: 0-8014-0537-8.

Recommended Reading Lists

Carlsen, G. Robert. *Books and the Teenage Reader, 2nd Revised Ed*. New York: Harper and Row, 1980. p.144. LC: 78-2117. ISBN: 0-06-010626-3.

Fiction for Youth: A Guide to Recommended Books, 2nd Ed. Ed. by Lillian Shapiro. New York: Neal-Schuman Publishers, Inc., 1986. pp. 164-165. LC: 85-18857. ISBN: 0-918212-94-4.

Gilbar, Steven. *Good Books: A Book Lover's Companion*. New Haven, CT: Ticknor & Fields, 1982. p. 159. LC: 82-5554. ISBN: 0-89919-127-4.

Good Reading: A Guide for Serious Readers, 21st Ed. Ed. by J. Sherwood Weber. New York: R. R. Bowker, 1978. p. 124. LC: 78-2424. ISBN: 0-8352-1063-4.

The Reader's Advisor: A Layman's Guide to Literature, 13th Ed. 3v. New York: R. R. Bowker, 1986. v.1 pp. 567-568. LC: 57-13277. ISBN: 0-8352-2145-8.

Books for the Teen Age, 1986. Office for Young Adult Services, New York Public Library.

Fiction Catalog, 11th Ed. Ed. by Juliette Yaakov. New York: H. W. Wilson, 1986. p. 531. LC: 85-32298. ISBN: 0-8242-0728-9.

Senior High School Catalog, 13th Ed. New York: H. W. Wilson, 1987. LC: 87-7377. ISBN: 0-8242-0755-6.

Happy Endings Are All Alike

By Sandra Scoppettone
New York: Harper and Row, 1978. LC: 78-2976. ISBN: 0025240-5.

Annotation

Although Scoppettone treats her controversial subjects--lesbianism and rape---with neither graphic language nor excessive didacticism, her novel has been the target of attack from its first publication. Some reviewers praised the book; others found it poorly written.

Linda Silver, for example, writing in *SLJ*, said: "While Peggy and Janet gush, coo, and spat in a manner that embarrasses more than it enlightens, the girls' families and friends serve as convenient exemplars of various attitudes toward lesbianism." She goes on to say: "The title is irrelevant to the story and the story is irrelevant to any understanding of lesbianism or rape, displaying a lack of integrity and a willingness to address the concerns and interests of young people simplistically, sensationally, and spuriously."

On the other hand, the novel is listed in publications by gays for gays as worthwhile and sensitive, and a review in the *Interracial Books for Children Bulletin* praises it for having the very qualities that Silver denies.

Scoppettone has presented frankly and honestly a kind of relationship which, though teachers and parents choose to look the other way and ignore, is often present in the teenage and the adult world. And she has done so sympathetically, and--despite Silver's negative description of it---realistically, Perhaps more important, she has shown us how society reacts to a lesbian relationship: families look the other way; boys feel justified in committing rape.

Happy Endings can help its readers to understand love in its varying manifestations. It is an "open" novel; that is, it calls on its readers to bring what they know and feel about love and hate to the act of reading it. The novel neither promotes nor condemns lesbianism; it merely recognizes that it occurs. But clearly the love between Peggy and Jane is valued; equally clearly, the hatred expressed by the rapist is condemned. The rape is an act of violence, and sexuality has nothing to do with it.

Perhaps, that, in the end, best explains the book. Sexuality has nothing to do with it. Rather, it is about love and hatred, and how in this instance, society rejects the love, and condones the hate.

Examples of Recent Challenges

Removed from the Evergreen School District of Vancouver, Washington (1983) along with twenty-nine other titles. The American Civil Liberties Union of Washington has filed suit contending that the removals constitute censorship, a violation of plaintiff's right to free speech and due process, and the acts are a violation of the state's Open Meetings Act because the removal decisions were made behind closed doors.

In Muncie, Indiana (1986) the book was placed on a restricted shelf in the school library after a school employee complained that it promoted lesbianism.

Sources: Office for Intellectual Freedom, American Library Association; and The People for the American Way.

Reviews

Catholic Library World. 50:117 (10/78). ISSN: 0008-820X.

Center for Children's Books Bulletin. 32:86 (1/79). ISSN: 0008-9036.

Interracial Books for Children. 10:16 (6/79). ISSN: 0146-5562.

Kirkus Reviews. 46:1022 (9/15/78). ISSN: 0042-6598.

Kliatt Young Adult Paperback Guide. 13:14 (Winter/80). ISSN: 0199-2376.

New York Times Book Review. (12/10/78). ISSN: 0028-7806.

Publishers Weekly. 214:100 (7/24/78). ISSN: 0000-0019.

School Library Journal. 25:65 (2/79). ISSN: 0000-0035.

Wilson Library Bulletin. 53:340-341 (12/78). ISSN: 0043-5651.

Standard Reference Sources 0091-3421.

Contemporary Literary Criticism. Detroit: Gale Research Company, 1983. v.26 pp. 400-405. LC: 76-38938. ISBN: 0-8103-4400-9. ISSN:

Something About the Author. Detroit: Gale Research Company, 1976. v.9 p. 162. LC: 72-27107. ISBN: 0-8103-0066-4.

Articles

DeLuca, Geraldine. "Taking true risks: controversial issues in new young adult novels." *The Lion and the Unicorn* 3:125-150 (Winter/79-80). ISSN: 0147-2593.

Wilson, David E. "The open library: YA books for gay teens." *English Journal* 73:60-63 (11/84). "Advocating YA novels with gay themes." *English Journal* 75:36-39 (4/86). ISSN: 0013-8274.

Recommended Reading Lists

Best Books for Young Adults 1978. Young Adult Services Division. Chicago: American Library Association, 1979.

Books for the Teenage 1979. Office of Young Adult Services. New York Public Library.

Books for You: A Booklist for Senior High School Students. Ed. by Robert Small, Jr. Committee on the Senior High School Booklist. Urbana, IL: National Council of Teachers of English, 1982. LC: 82-8199. ISBN: 0-8141-0359-6.

Carlsen, G. Robert. *Books and the Teenage Reader, 2nd Revised Ed*. New York: Harper and Row, 1980. p. 75. LC: 78-2117. ISBN: 0-06-010626-3.

Dreyer, Sharon Spredemann. *The Bookfinder: A Guide to Children's Literature About the Needs and Problems of Youth Aged 2-15*. 3v. Circle Pines, MN: American Guidance Service, dates vary. v.2 (1981) #578. LC: 78-105919. ISBN: 0-913476-46-3.

New Paperbacks for Young Adults: A Thematic Guide, 2nd Ed. Ed. by Fay Blostein. Toronto: Ontario Library Association, 1981. ISBN: 0-88969-024-3.

Of Mice and Men

By John Steinbeck

New York: Covici Friede, 1937. LC: 37-2568.
New York: Modern Library, 1938. LC: 38-6023 ISBN: 0-394-60472-5.
New York: Bantam Books, 1970 ISBN: 0-553-26675-6.

Annotation

Of Mice and Men is the story of the friendship between two itinerant California laborers, George and Lennie. George protects Lennie, a large and powerful but mentally disabled man, from the harassment and cruel teasing of those who are too ignorant to know better. George and Lennie's dream is to find a place of their own, where they can live in peace and dignity, but this dream is shattered by Lennie's innocent violence. The story ends when George must kill Lennie to save him from an ignoble death at the hands of a lynch mob led by the husband of a woman Lennie killed unintentionally.

Steinbeck's short novel is considered an American classic. It has been a standard on high school required reading lists for several generations. The play was voted the best of the 1938 season by the New York Drama Critics Circle; a 1939 film version was similarly praised, and retains its luster even today. In 1981 the play was redone for television and again won critical acclaim.

Its value for high school students lies not only in its sensitive portrayal of innocence betrayed, but in its eloquent brevity, the biblical origins of its themes, and its emotional power. Two main elements of the story, the mentally disabled protagonist, and the violence of the action, have proved to be controversial. Yet for these very reasons, the book lends itself to vigorous critical discussion.

Of Mice and Men is particularly appropriate to stimulate an examination of such issues as personal responsibility, the nature and obligations of friendship, and the biblical question: Am I my brother's keeper?

Steinbeck wrote *Of Mice and Men* first in novella form, then adapted it as a play, which was produced on Broadway in 1937 and won critical acclaim; it was published first in dramatic form, and then as a novella. A feature film was made in 1939, directed by Lewis Milestone and distributed by Corinth Films. The play was produced for television in 1981, directed by Reza Badiyi.

Examples of Recent Challenges

Banned in Syracuse, Indiana (1974), Oil City, Pennsylvania (1977), Grand Blanc, Michigan (1979) and Continental, Ohio (1980).

Challenged in Greenville, South Carolina (1977) by the Fourth Province of the Knights of the Ku Klux Klan; in the Vernon-Verona-Sherill, New York school district (1980); St. David, Arizona

(1981), and Tell City, Indiana (1982) due to "profanity and using God's name in vain."

Banned from classroom use at the Scottsboro, Alabama Skyline High School (1983) due to "profanity." The chairman of the Knoxville, Tennessee School Board vowed to have "filthy books" removed from Knoxville's public schools (1984), and picked Steinbeck's novel as the first target due to "its vulgar language."

Source: The Office for Intellectual Freedom, American Library Association.

Reviews

Booklist. 33:276 (5/39). ISSN: 0006-7385.

Chicago Daily Tribune. (2/27/37).

Manchester Guardian. (9/14/37). ISSN: 0025-2004.

Nation. 144:275 (3/6/37). ISSN: 0027-8378.

New Republic. 90:118 (3/3/37). ISSN: 0028-6583.

New York Times. (2/28/37). ISSN: 0028-7806.

North American Review. 243:406-413 (6/37). ISSN: 0029-2397.

Saturday Review of Literature. 15:7 (2/27/37). ISSN: 0361-1655.

Times Literary Supplement. (10/2/37). ISSN: 0307-6614.

Wilson Library Bulletin. 33:100 (5/37). ISSN: 0043-5651.

Yale Review. 26:vi (Summer/37). ISSN: 0044-0124.

Standard Reference Sources

Contemporary Literary Criticism. Detroit: Gale Research Company, 1976. v.5 pp. 406-409. LC: 76-389838. ISBN: 0-8103-0108-3. v.21 pp. 366, 372, 378-386, 389-392. LC: 76-389838. ISBN: 0-8103-0117-2.

Dictionary of Literary Biography, V.7: Twentieth Century American Dramatists, Part 2: K-Z. Ed. by John MacNicholas. Detroit: Gale Research Company, 1981. pp. 271-276. ISBN: 0-8103-0928-9.

1300 Critical Evaluations of Selected Novels and Plays. Ed. by Frank Magill. Englewood Cliffs, NJ: Salem Press, 1976. v.3 p. 1606. LC: 78-55387. ISBN: 0-89356-046-4.

Miscellaneous Discussion

Benson, Jackson J. *The True Adventures of John Steinbeck, Writer: A Biography.* New York: Viking Press, 1984. LC: 82-17534. ISBN: 0-670-16685-5.

Jain, Sunita. *John Steinbeck's Concept of Man: A Critical Study of His Novels.* New Delhi: New Statesman Publishing Co., 1979; Atlantic Highlands, NJ: Humanities Press, 1980. LC: 79-904006. ISBN: 0-391-01730-6.

Levant, Howard. *The Novels of John Steinbeck: A Critical Study.* Columbia, MO: University of Missouri Press, 1975. LC: 74-76251. ISBN: 0-8262-0424-4.

Owens, Leslie. "*Of Mice and Men*: the dreams of commitment." In *Modern Critical Views: John Steinbeck.* Ed. by Harold Bloom. New York: Chelsea House, 1987. pp. 145-149. LC: 86-29958. ISBN: 0-87754-635-5.

Steinbeck: A Collection of Critical Essays. Ed. by Robert M. Davis. Englewood Cliffs, NJ: Prentice-Hall, 1972. LC: 75-178763. ISBN: 0-13-846659-9.

Awards and Prizes

Best Play, New York Drama Critics Circle Award 1938.
Nobel Prize for Literature, 1962. For the body of his work.

Recommended Reading Lists

Books for the Teen Age, 1983. New York Public Library.

Books for You: A Booklist for Senior High School Students. Ed. by Kenneth Donelson. National Council of Teachers of English. New York: Scholastic Books, 1976. p. 97. LC: 76-41688. ISBN: 0-8141-0362-6.

Carlsen, G. Robert. *Books and the Teenage Reader, 2nd Revised Ed.* New York: Harper and Row, 1980. p. 145. LC: 78-2117. ISBN: 0-06-010626-3.

Fiction Catalog, 11th Ed. Ed. by Juliette Yaakov. New York: H. W. Wilson, 1986. p. 578. LC: 85-32298. ISBN: 0-8242-0728-9.

Fiction for Youth: A Guide to Recommended Books, 2nd Ed. Ed. by Lillian Shapiro. New York: Neal-Schuman Publishers, Inc., 1986. pp. 182-183. LC: 85-18857. ISBN: 0-918212-94-4.

Gilbar, Steven. *Good Books: A Book Lover's Companion.* New York: Ticknor & Fields, 1982. p. 185. LC: 82-5554. ISBN: 0-89919-127-4.

Outstanding Books for the College Bound. Young Adult Services Division. Chicago: American Library Association, 1984. p. 12. LC: 83-25714. ISBN: 0-8389-3302-5.

The Reader's Advisor: A Layman's Guide to Literature, 13th Ed. 3v. New York: R. R. Bowker, 1986. v.1 pp. 571-572. LC: 57-13277. ISBN: 0-8352-2145-8.

Senior High School Catalog, 13th Ed. New York: H. W. Wilson, 1987. p. 191. LC: 87-7377. ISBN: 0-8242-0755-6.

Walker, Elinor. *Doors to More Mature Reading: Detailed Notes on Adult Books for Use with Young People, 2nd Ed.* Chicago: American Library Association, 1981. LC: 81-17615. ISBN: 0-8389-03440-4.

The Adventures of Huckleberry Finn: Tom Sawyer's Companion

By Mark Twain (Samuel Langhorne Clemens)
illustrated by Edward Windsor Kemble.
London: Chatto & Windus, 1884; New York: C.L. Webster, 1885.
(facsimile of first ed.) *The Art of Huckleberry Finn: Text, Sources, Criticism*. Ed. by Hamlin Hill and Walter Blair. San Francisco: Chandler Publishing, 1962. LC: 62-11841.

Annotation

Huckleberry Finn is generally recognized as a comic and biting condemnation of the callousness of a society that pretended to value virtue while condoning slavery. Huck, though crude and unpolished by society's standards, has the moral strength to do what he is convinced is right. He helps the slave Jim escape, even though it means breaking the law, and even if it means going to Hell. Huck's kindness and integrity, and Jim's generosity and dignity, present a striking contrast to the meanness, corruption and deceit of the so-called civilized folks with which they meet as they travel down the Mississippi River.

Most scholars of American literature consider *The Adventures of Huckleberry Finn* to be one of the three or four masterpieces of American literature. *The Scarlet Letter* and *Moby Dick* are the others most frequently listed. Many authors have praised the novel, including T. S. Eliot and Ernest Hemingway, and have admitted to being influenced by Twain in their own works. Hemingway went so far as to declare that all of contemporary American literature derives from *Huckleberry Finn*. (See Kaplan, *Born to Trouble*, page 10.)

Although when first published it was criticized as profane and setting a vulgar example for young and impressionable readers, and in our own time condemned by some black parents and educators who find it racist and demeaning, and complain that the character of Jim presents an embarrassing and negative image of their race to black children, both scholars and generations of thoughtful readers have been moved by the story and the decency of Huck and Jim. It is considered by many to be the quintessential depiction of the American character, faithfully delineating both its native virtues and its deepest flaws.

There have been a number of film, television, and staged versions of Twain's masterpiece. The Paramount production in 1931, directed by Norman Taurog, featured James (Junior) Durkin as Huck and Clarence Muse as Jim. In 1939, Joseph L. Mankiewicz produced what is still considered the best version of *Huckleberry Finn* for MGM, directed by Richard Thorpe and starring Mickey Rooney as Huck and Rex Ingram as Jim. A 1960 remake by MGM was produced by Samuel Goldwyn, Jr. and directed by Michael Curtiz, with Eddie Hodges as Huck and Archie Moore as Jim. United Artists did a disappointing musical version of the story in 1974, produced by Arthur P. Jacobs, directed by J. Lee Thompson, with Jeff East as Huck and Paul Winfield as Jim. In 1975 ABC Circle Films did a "made for television" film, produced by Steven North, directed by Robert Tottem, and starring Ron Howard as Huck and Antonio Fargas as Jim. Most recently, a musical version of *Huckleberry Finn* called *Big River* (music and lyrics by Roger Miller, book by William Hauptman) was produced on Broadway in 1985 and won seven Tony Awards.

Examples of Recent Challenges

Banned in Concord, Massachusetts (1885) as "trash and suitable only for the slums"; excluded from the children's room of the Brooklyn, New York Public Library (1905) on the grounds that "Huck not only itched but scratched, and that he said sweat when he should have said perspiration."

Dropped from the New York City (1957) list of approved books for senior and junior high schools, partly because of objections to frequent use of the term "nigger."

Removed from the Miami-Dade County, Florida Junior College required reading list (1969) because the book "creates an emotional block for black students that inhibits learning."

Challenged as a "racist" novel in Winnetka, Illinois (1976), Warrington, Pennsylvania (1981), Davenport, Iowa (1981), Fairfax County, Virginia (1982), Houston, Texas (1982), State College, Pennsylvania Area School District (1983), Springfield, Illinois (1984), Waukegan, Illinois (1984).

Lakeland, Florida (1987) NAACP demanded that *Huckleberry Finn* be dropped from a high school English class, and that the book be removed from all schools throughout the county because of "racism."

Sources: The Office for Intellectual Freedom, American Library Association; and The People for the American Way.

Reviews

The original publication of *The Adventures of Huckleberry Finn* met with very mixed reviews. Some reviewers recognized its brilliance immediately; others were shocked by what they considered irreverence, and fussed over the bad grammar, "coarse expressions" and unexemplary behavior of its narrator and hero, Huck.

The fact is that, from its first publication, *Huckleberry Finn* was controversial. The earliest objections are interesting, though perhaps not especially relevant to contemporary challenges, since those early critics were white, middle class adults who saw Huck as an appallingly low class role model for their children.

Excerpts from the early reviews are included in several of the reference sources and books listed below. Since these sources and books are more easily accessed than the original review sources, we recommend them to fill the need for reviews.

In the introduction to *One Hundred Years of "Huckleberry Finn,"* John C. Gerber summarizes the early reviews and critical articles as follows:

"Some fifty articles on *Huckleberry Finn* appeared before 1920, many of them reviews published in the late 1880s. . . Writers of the period tended to address themselves to questions concerning the overall worth of the book and often came up with absurdly contradictory judgments. Consider a few examples of the questions raised and the contrary opinions voiced: Is *Huckleberry Finn* a work of art? (Yes, it is a literary masterpiece; no, it is trash.) Is the narrative true to life? (Yes, it is highly realistic; no, it is no more truthful than a dime novel.) Is the humor of high quality? (Yes, it is the finest that has appeared in America; no, it is coarse, flat, dated and grotesque.)" (page 6)

Standard Reference Sources

Twentieth Century Literary Criticism. Editors vary. Detroit: Gale Research Company, dates vary.
v.6 pp. 452-488 (1982) LC: 76-46132 ISBN: 0-8103-0180-6
v.12 pp. 423-455 (1984) LC: 76-46132 ISBN: 0-8103-0223-3
v.19 pp.*349-417 (1986) LC: 76-46132 ISBN: 0-8103-2401-6

*The entry in v.19 is devoted exclusively to excerpts from critical essays and analyses of *Huckleberry Finn*.

Yesterday's Authors of Books for Children. Ed. by Anne Commire. Detroit: Gale Research Company, 1978. v.2 pp. 50-83. LC: 76-17501. ISBN: 0-8103-0073-3.

Miscellaneous Discussion

Because Mark Twain is one of the three or four most important figures in American literature, biographical information concerning him, his literary and philosophical aims and opinions, are available in many sources. The biographies listed below are standard works:

Hill, Hamlin. *Mark Twain: God's Fool.* New York: Harper & Row, 1973. LC: 72-9754. ISBN: 0-06-011893-8.

Kaplan, Justin. *Mark Twain and His World.* New York: Simon and Schuster, 1974. LC: 72-87659. ISBN: 0-671-21462-4.

Kaplan, Justin. *Mr. Clemens and Mark Twain: A Biography.* New York: Simon and Schuster, 1966. LC: 66-17603. ISBN: 0-671-20-202-5.

Smith, Henry Nash. *Mark Twain: The Development of a Writer*. Cambridge, MA: Harvard University Press, 1962. LC: 62-19224. ISBN: 0-674-54875-2.

The following are standard critical analyses of Twain's work:

Blair, Walter. *Mark Twain and Huckleberry Finn*. Berkeley, CA: University of California Press, 1960. LC: 59-15693. ISBN: 0-520-02521-0.

Eliot, T. S. "An introduction to *Huckleberry Finn*." In *Adventures of Huckleberry Finn: An Authoritative Text, Backgrounds and Sources, Criticism, 2nd Ed.* Ed. by Sculley Bradley, et al. New York: W. W. Norton, 1977. pp. 328-335. LC: 76-30648. ISBN: 0-393-04454-8.

Hearn, Michael Patrick. *The Annotated Huckleberry Finn*. New York: Clarkson N. Potter, Inc., 1981. LC: 81-5904. ISBN: 0-517-533031-7.

Kaplan, Justin. *Born to Trouble: One Hundred Years of Huckleberry Finn*. Washington: Library of Congress, 1985. ISBN: 0-8444-0494-2.

Kazin, Alfred. *An American Procession*. New York: Knopf, 1984. pp. 181-210. LC: 83-26843. ISBN: 0-394-50378-3.

Sattelmeyer, Robert and J. Donald Crowley, Eds. *One Hundred Years of "Huckleberry Finn": The Boy, His Book, and American Culture*. Columbia, MO: University of Missouri Press, 1985. LC: 84-19574. ISBN: 0-8262-0457-0.

Trilling, Lionel. *The Liberal Imagination*. New York: Harcourt, Brace, Jovanovich, 1979, c.1950. pp. 104-117. LC: 78-65749. ISBN: 0-15-151197-7.

Recommended Reading Lists

Suggested reading lists for secondary students almost without exception list *The Adventures of Huckleberry Finn* as a work of literature that all students should have read by the time they complete high school. The following are some examples of those many lists of recommended reading on which the novel appears:

Books for the Teen Age, 1986. Office of Young Adult Services, New York Public Library.

Books for You: A Booklist for Senior High School Students. Ed. by Robert C. Small, Jr. Committee on the Senior High School Booklist. Urbana, IL: National Council of Teachers of English, 1982. LC: 82-8199. ISBN: 0-8141-0359-6.

Fiction Catalog, 11th Ed. Ed. by Juliette Yaakov. New York: H. W. Wilson, 1986. p. 618. LC: 85-32298. ISBN: 0-8242-0728-9.

Junior High School Catalog, 5th Ed. New York: H. W. Wilson, 1985. LC: 85-17934. ISBN: 0-8242-0720-3.

Outstanding Books for the College Bound. Ed. by Mary Ann Paulin and Susan Berlin. Young Adult Services Division. Chicago: American Library Association, 1984. LC: 83-25714. ISBN: 0-8389-3302-5.

Your Reading: A Booklist for Junior High and Middle School Students. Ed. by Jane Christensen. Committee on the Junior High and Middle School Booklist. Urbana, IL: National Council of Teachers of English, 1983. LC: 83-17426. ISBN: 0-8141-5938-9.

Articles

"Black writers on Huckleberry Finn." *Mark Twain Journal* 22:1-52 (Fall/84). ISSN: 0025-3499. (special issue)

Cloonan, M. V. "Censorship of *The Adventures of Huckleberry Finn:* an investigation." *Top of the News* 40:189-196 (Winter/84). ISSN: 0040-9286.

Slaughterhouse Five;
Or, The Children's Crusade

By Kurt Vonnegut

New York: Delacorte Press, 1969. LC: 69-11929.

Annotation

Slaughterhouse Five raises disturbing questions of morality versus power. The main protagonist, Billy Pilgrim, optometrist and World War II veteran, takes us on a "trip" to Dresden during the war and to the alien planet of Tralfamdore.

We learn that Billy has suffered a breakdown and has been hospitalized by his daughter. He is kidnapped and transported to Tralfamdore, where he is mated with Montana Wildhack. The trip to Tralfamdore is Billy's escape from the horrors he witnessed during the Dresden bombing.

The struggles of conscience to reconcile the horrors carried out in the course of waging war with the principles which the war is ostensibly fought to defend, is revealed in this anti-war novel of the seventies. "So it goes," is the call sign of our hero throughout this laid back satire.

After the burning of the book by the Drake, North Dakota School Board in 1973, Vonnegut responded:

"If you were to bother to read my books, to behave as educated persons would, you would learn that they are not sexy, and do not argue in favor of wildness of any kinds. They beg that people be kinder and more responsible than they often are. It is true that some characters speak coarsely. That is because people speak coarsely in real life. Especially soldiers and hard-working men speak coarsely, and even our most sheltered children know that. . ." (Ziegfeld, Richard E. "Kurt Vonnegut on censorship and moral values." *Modern Fiction Studies* 26:631-635 (Winter/80-81) Purdue Research Foundation, West Lafayette, IN 47907.)

Examples of Recent Challenges

Challenged in many communities, but burned in Drake, North Dakota (1973). Banned in Rochester, Michigan (1972) because the novel "contains and makes references to religious matters" and thus fell within the ban of the establishment clause. An appellate court upheld its usage in the school in Todd v. Rochester Community Schools, 41 Mich. App. 320, 200 N.W.2d 90 (1972).

Banned in Levittown, New York (1975), North Jackson, Ohio (1979), and Lakeland, Florida (1982) because of the "book's explicit sexual scenes, violence, and obscene language."

Barred from purchase at the Washington Park High School in Racine, Wisconsin (1984) by the district administrative assistant for instructional services. Challenged at the Owensburo, Kentucky

High School library (1985) because of "foul language, a section depicting a picture of an act of bestiality, a reference to 'Magic Fingers' attached to the protagonist's bed to help him sleep," and the sentence: "The gun made a ripping sound like the opening of the fly of God Almighty."

Restricted to students who have parental permission at the four Racine, Wisconsin Unified District high school libraries (1986) because of "language used in the book, depictions of torture, ethnic slurs, and negative portrayals of women."

Challenged in the La Rue County, Kentucky high school library (1987) by parents who objected that the book was "undermining Christian faith, glorifying death and containing profanity."

Sources: Office for Intellectual Freedom, American Library Association; and The People for the American Way.

Reviews

American Scholar. 38:718 (Autumn/69). ISSN: 0003-0937.

Atlantic. 223:145 (4/69). ISSN: 0004-6795.

Best Sellers. 29:31 (4/15/69). ISSN: 0005-9625.

Christian Century. 86:1069 (8/13/69). ISSN: 0009-5281.

Christian Science Monitor. 61:15 (4/17/69).

Commonweal. 90:347 (6/6/69). ISSN: 0010-3330.

Library Journal. 94:1021 (3/1/69); 94:4624 (12/15/69). ISSN: 0363-0277.

Nation. 208:736 (6/9/69). ISSN: 0037-8378.

New Republic. 160:33 (4/26/69). ISSN: 0028-6583.

New York Times Book Review. (4/6/69); (10/20/85). ISSN: 0028-7806.

New Yorker. 45:145 (5/17/69). ISSN: 0028-792X.

Newsweek. 73:122 (4/14/69). ISSN: 0028-9604.

Saturday Review. 52:25 (3/29/69). ISSN: 0091-620X.

Time. 93:106 (4/11/69). ISSN: 0040-781X.

Washington Post Book World. (4/13/69). ISSN: 0006-7369.

Standard Reference Sources

Contemporary Authors, New Revision Series. Detroit: Gale Research Company, 1981. v.1 pp. 678-684. LC: 62-52046. ISBN: 0-8103-1930-6.

Contemporary Literary Criticism. Editors vary. Detroit: Gale Research Company, dates vary.
v.1 pp. 347-348 (1973) LC: 76-38938 ISBN: 0-8103-0100-8

v.2 pp. 451-456 (1974) LC: 76-38938 ISBN: 0-8103-0102-4
v.3 pp. 494-506 (1975) LC: 76-38938 ISBN: 0-8103-0104-0
v.4 pp. 460-470 (1974) LC: 76-38938 ISBN: 0-8103-0106-7
v.5 pp. 464-471 (1976) LC: 76-38938 ISBN: 0-8103-0108-3
v.8 pp. 529-535 (1978) LC: 76-38938 ISBN: 0-8103-0114-8
v.12 pp. 600-630 (1980) LC: 76-38938 ISBN: 0-8103-0122-9
v.22 pp. 444-452 (1982) LC: 76-38938 ISBN: 0-8103-0115-6

Current Biography Yearbook/1970. Ed. by Charles Moritz. New York: H. W. Wilson, 1971. pp. 429-432. LC: 40-47432. ISBN: 0-8242-0404-2.

Dictionary of Literary Biography, V.8: Twentieth Century American Science Fiction Writers, Part 2: M-Z. Ed. by David Cowart and Thomas L. Wymer. Detroit: Gale Research Company, 1981. pp. 184-190. LC: 81-4182. ISBN: 0-8103-0918-1.

Who's Who in America, 1987-1988, 139th Ed. New York: St. Martin's Press, 1987. LC: 87-16933. ISBN: 0-312-00236-X.

Articles

Bianculli, David. "A Kurt post-mortem on the generally eclectic theater." *Film Comment* 21:41 (12/85). ISSN: 0015-119X.

Blackford, R. "Physics and fantasy: scientific mysticism, Kurt Vonnegut, and *Gravity's Rainbow*." *Journal of Popular Culture* 19:35-44 (Winter/85). ISSN: 0022-3340.

"Censorship in U.S. and Canada." *New York Times* (1/16/86).

"Facts worse than death." *North American Review* 267:46-49 (12/82). ISSN: 0029-1012.

Gill, R. B. "Bargaining in good faith: the laughter of Vonnegut, Grass, and Dundera." *Critique* 25:77-91 (Winter/84). ISSN: 0735-6501.

Giannone, R. "Violence in the fiction of Kurt Vonnegut." *Thought* 56:58-76 (3/81). ISSN: 0040-6457.

Hartsthorne, Thomas. "From *Catch-22* to *Slaughterhouse V*." *South Atlantic Quarterly* 78:17-33 (I/1979). ISSN: 0038-2876.

Hume, K. "Kurt Vonnegut and the myths and symbols of meaning." *Texas Studies in Literature and Language* 24:429-447 (Winter/82). ISSN: 0040-4691.

"Hypocrites you always have with you." *Nation* 230:469-470 (4/19/80). ISSN: 0027-8378.

"Interview of Vonnegut by Buckley." *New York Times* (1/12/86).

"Kurt Vonnegut comments on past censorship of his book." *New York Times* (1/12/86).

Matheson, T. J. "This lousy little book: the genesis and development of *Slaughterhouse-five* as revealed in chapter one." *Studies in the Novel* 16:228-240 (Summer/84). ISSN: 0039-3827.

"MCLU survey finds censorship in Minnesota 'appalling'." *Library Journal* 74:386 (2/15/82). ISSN: 0363-0277.

Musil, Robert K. "There must be more to love than death: a conversation with Kurt Vonnegut." *Nation* 231:128 (8/2/80). ISSN: 0027-8378.

Nuwer, H. "Kurt Vonnegut close up." *Saturday Evening Post* 258:38-39 (5-6/86). ISSN: 0048-9239.

"Reluctant big shot." *Nation* 232:282 (3/7/81). ISSN: 0027-8378.

"Truly modern hero." *Psychology Today* 15:9-10 (8/81). ISSN: 0033-3107.

Veix, Donald B. "Teaching a censored novel: *Slaughterhouse-five*." *English Journal* 64:25 (10/75). ISSN: 0013-8274.

"Vonnegut: the fundamental piece of obscenity." *Publishers Weekly* 229:263 (1/31/86). ISSN: 0000-0019.

"War preparers anonymous." (Excerpt from address on 1/17/84) *Harper's* 268:41 (3/84). ISSN: 0017-789X.

Ziegfeld, R. E. "Kurt Vonnegut on censorship and moral values." *Modern Fiction Studies* 26:631-635 (Winter/80-81). ISSN: 0026-7724.

Miscellaneous Discussion

Goldsmith, David H. *Kurt Vonnegut: Fantasist of Fire and Ice.* Bowling Green, OH: Bowling Green University Press, 1972. LC: 75-186633. ISBN: 0-87972-024-7.

Klinkowitz, Jerome. *Kurt Vonnegut.* New York: Methuen, 1982. LC: 81-22558. ISBN: 0-416-33480-6.

Lundquist, James. *Kurt Vonnegut.* New York: Frederick Ungar, 1977. LC: 76-15654. ISBN: 0-8044-2564-7.

Mayo, Clark. *Kurt Vonnegut: The Gospel from Outer Space; Or, Yes We Have No Nirvanas.* San Bernardino, CA: Borgo Press, 1977. LC: 77-24460. ISBN: 0-89370-111-4.

The Vonnegut Statement. Ed. by Jerome Klinkowitz and John Somer. New York: Delacorte Press, 1973. LC: 72-5161. ISBN: none listed.

Recommended Reading Lists

Carlsen, G. Robert. *Books and the Teenage Reader, 2nd Revised Ed.* New York: Harper and Row, 1980. p. 276. LC: 78-2117. ISBN: 0-06-010626-3.

Fiction Catalog, 11th Ed. Ed. by Juliette Yaakov. New York: H. W. Wilson, 1986. p. 636. LC: 85-32298. ISBN: 0-8242-0728-9.

Fiction for Youth: A Guide to Recommended Books, 2nd Ed. Ed. by Lillian Shapiro. New York: Neal-Schuman Publishers, Inc., 1986. p. 195. LC: 85-18857. ISBN: 0-918212-94-4.

Gilbar, Steven. *Good Books: A Book Lover's Companion.* New Haven, CT: Ticknor & Fields, 1982. p. 370. LC: 82-5554. ISBN: 0-89919-127-4.

Good Reading: A Guide for Serious Readers, 21st Ed. Ed. by J. Sherwood Weber. New York: R. R. Bowker, 1978. p. 124. LC: 78-2424. ISBN: 0-8352-1063-4.

The Reader's Advisor: A Layman's Guide to Literature, 13th Ed. 3v. New York: R. R. Bowker, 1986. v.1 pp. 577-578. LC: 57-13277. ISBN: 0-8352-2145-8.

Senior High School Library Catalog, 13th Ed. New York: H. W. Wilson, 1987. LC: 87-7377. ISBN: 0-8242-0755-6.

The Color Purple

By Alice Walker

New York: Harcourt, Brace, Jovanovich, 1982. LC: 81-48242. ISBN: 0-15-119153-0.

Annotation

Reading and re-reading *The Color Purple*, one passage seems to illuminate the intent or purpose of Walker's story of two sisters, bound to each other by love and fear, joy and sorrow, and reunited after a separation of thirty years.

"He laugh. Who you think you is? he say. You can't curse nobody. Look at you. You black, you pore, you ugly, you a woman. Goddam, he say, you nothing at all." (*The Color Purple*, p. 176)

That is what people fear and despise in this book. For people who believe, implicitly, that to be black/poor/ugly/woman is to be nothing---and to be all of these together is to be less than nothing, the lowest thing in Creation---Walker's book is political, social and sexual heresy.

For Walker is blaspheming against the accepted order of things. She is daring to say that you can be black/poor/ugly/woman and you are nonetheless somebody, a person of intrinsic dignity and worth. There is no such thing as "trash" if you believe, and practice the belief (in Shug's words) that God is not He or She but It, and that it is everywhere and in everything.

"I'm pore, I'm black, I may be ugly and can't cook, a voice says to everything listening. But I'm here." (*The Color Purple*, p. 176)

There is nothing new or shocking in the elements of Walker's narrative. We have heard all of these stories before. It is the angle of approach that is so unsettling. We have all heard about oppression from the point-of-view of the oppressors, about racial relations from the dominant race, about religion from those who preach God the Old Man, about marriage from husbands and sex from men. But in *The Color Purple* we view these familiar conflicts from the other perspective, from the inside out and the bottom up, and what we are forced to see is painful indeed.

Yet out of violence, poverty, oppression and abuse, Celie creates a life for herself and reaches out with love to those around her. Out of all she has experienced she emerges strong and enduring. Quilting is the metaphor for this process of growth in the book: Celie takes the ragged scraps of her life and pieces them together with exquisite stitches into a pattern of beauty. For Walker, Celie's life, like her quilts, is beautiful and precious because of the time and effort, the thought and care, which have gone into its making.

A film of this novel was made in 1985 by Warner Brothers; directed by Steven Spielberg, and starring Danny Glover, Whoopi

Goldberg as Celie, Margaret Avery and Oprah Winfrey. It was nominated for eleven Academy Awards.

Examples of Recent Challenges

Challenged as an appropriate reading for an Oakland, California high school honors class (1984) due to the work's "sexual and social explicitness" and its "troubling ideas about race relations, man's relationship to God, African history and human sexuality." After nine months of haggling and delays, a divided Oakland Board of Education gave formal approval for the book's use.

Rejected for purchase by the Hayward, California school trustees (1985) because of "rough language" and "explicit sex scenes."

Removed from the open shelves of the Newport News, Virginia school library (1986) because of its "profanity and sexual references" and because the school principal felt it "might incite rape." The book was restricted to a special section accessible only to students over the age of eighteen or those who have written permission from a parent.

Sources: Office for Intellectual Freedom, American Library Association; and The People for the American Way.

Reviews

Black Enterprise. 12:30 (12/82). ISSN: 0006-4165.

Booklist. 78:1042 (4/15/82). ISSN: 0006-7385.

Boston Review. 7:29 (10/82). ISSN: 0734-2306.

Commonweal. 110:93-94 (2/11/83). ISSN: 0010-5330.

Essence. 13:20 (10/82). ISSN: 0014-0880.

Kirkus Reviews. 50:518 (4/15/82). ISSN: 0042-6598.

Library Journal. 107:1115 (6/1/82). ISSN: 0363-0277.

Nation. 235:181-184 (9/4/82); 235:696 (12/25/82). ISSN: 0027-8378.

New York Review of Books. 29:35-36 (8/12/82). ISSN: 0028-7504.

New York Times Book Review. (7/25/82); 88:19 (5/29/83). ISSN: 0028-7806.

New Yorker. 58:106 (9/6/82). ISSN: 0028-792X.

Newsweek. 99:67-68 (6/21/82). ISSN: 0028-9604.

San Francisco Review of Books. 7:5 (Summer/82); 7:23 (1/83).

Washington Post Book World. (7/25/82). ISSN: 0006-7369.

West Coast Review of Books. 8:22 (9/82). ISSN: 0095-3555.

Reference Sources

American Women Writers: A Critical Reference Guide, from Colonial Times to the Present. 4v. Ed. by Lina Mainiers. New York: Frederick Ungar, 1982. pp. 313-315. LC: 78-20945. ISBN: 0-8044-3151-5.

Dictionary of Literary Biography; Volume Six: American Novelists Since World War II, Second Series. Ed. by James E. Kibler, Jr. Detroit: Gale Research Company, 1980. pp. 350-358. LC: 80-22495. ISBN: 0-8103-0908-4.

Dictionary of Literary Biography; Volume Thirty-Three: Afro-American Fiction Writers After 1955. Ed. by Thadious M. Davis and Trudier Harris. Detroit: Gale Research Company, 1984. pp. 258-271. LC: 84-18724. ISBN: 0-8103-1711-7.

Contemporary Authors, First Revision Series. Detroit: Gale Research Company, 1979. v.37-40 pp. 582-583. LC: 62-52046. ISBN: 0-8103-0040-0.

Contemporary Authors, New Revision Series. Detroit: Gale Research Company, 1983. v.9 pp. 514-517. LC: 81-640179. ISBN: 0-8103-1938-1.

Contemporary Literary Criticism. Editors vary. Detroit: Gale Research Company, dates vary.

v.5	pp. 476-477	(1976)	LC: 76-38938	ISBN: 0-8103-0108-3
v.6	pp. 553-554	(1976)	LC: 76-38938	ISBN: 0-8103-0110-5
v.9	pp. 557-558	(1978)	LC: 76-38938	ISBN: 0-8103-0116-4
v.27	pp. 448-454	(1984)	LC: 76-38938	ISBN: 0-8103-4401-7
v.46	pp. 422-432	(1988)	LC: 76-38938	ISBN: 0-8103-4420-3

Something About the Author. Ed. by Anne Commire. Detroit: Gale Research Company, 1983. v.31 pp. 177-179. LC: 72-27107. ISBN: 0-8103-0057-5.

Articles

Bradley, D. "Telling the black woman's story." *New York Times Magazine* 133:24-37 (1/8/84).

Harris, Trudier. "On *The Color Purple*, stereotypes, and silence." *Black American Literature Forum* 18:155-161 (Winter/84). ISSN: 0148-6179.

Pinckney, D. "Black victims, black villains." *New York Review of Books* 34:17-20 (1/29/87). ISSN: 0028-7504.

Stade, George. "Womanist fiction and male characters." *Partisan Review* 52:264-270 (1985). ISSN: 0031-2525.

Steinem, Gloria. "Do you know this woman? She knows you: a profile of Alice Walker." *Ms.* 10:35-37, 89-94 (6/82). ISSN: 0047-8318.

Walker, Alice. "Finding Celie's voice." *Ms.* 14:71-72+ (12/85). ISSN: 0047-8318.

Washington, Mary Helen. "Alice Walker: her mother's gifts." *Ms.*

10:38 (6/82). ISSN: 0047-8318.

Wesley, Richard. "*The Color Purple* debate: reading between the lines." *Ms.* 15:62, 90-92 (9/86). ISSN: 0047-8318.

Miscellaneous Discussion

Cook, Michael G. "Alice Walker." In *Afro-American Literature in the Twentieth Century; the Achievement of Intimacy.* New Haven, CT: Yale University Press, 1984. pp. 133-176. LC: 84-5066. ISBN: 0-300-03218-8.

Davis, T. M. "Alice Walker's celebration of self in southern generations." In *Women Writers of the Contemporary South.* Ed. by Peggy Whitman Prenshaw. Jackson, MS: University Press of Mississippi, 1984. pp. 39-53. LC: 84-5165. ISBN: 0-87805-222-4.

Dixon, Melvin. "Keep me from sinking down: Zora Neale Hurston, Alice Walker and Gayl Jones." In *Ride Out of the Wilderness; Geography and Identity in Afro-American Literature.* Champaign, IL: University of Illinois Press, 1987. pp. 83-120. LC: 86-30918. ISBN: 0-252-01414-6.

Fifer, E. "Alice Walker: the dialect and letters of *The Color Purple.*" In *Contemporary American Women Writers; Narrative Strategies.* Ed. by Catherine Rainwater and William J. Scheick. Lexington, KY: University Press of Kentucky, 1985. pp. 155-171. LC: 85-9116. ISBN: 0-8131-1558-2.

Light, A. "Fear of the happy ending: *The Color Purple,* reading and racism." In *Essays and Studies, Volume Forty: Broadening the Context.* Ed. by Michael Green in association with Richard Haggart, for the English Association. Atlantic Highlands, NJ: Humanities Press, 1987. pp. 103-117. LC: 36-8431.

Parker-Smith, Bettye J. "Alice Walker's women: in search of some peace of mind." In *Black Women Writers, 1950-1980: A Critical Evaluation.* Ed. by Mari Evans. Garden City, NY: Doubleday, 1984. pp. 478-493. LC: 81-43914. ISBN: 0-385-17124-2.

Pratt, L.H. and Darwell Pratt. *Alice Walker: A Bibliography.* Westport, CT: Meckler Corp., 1987. ISBN: 0-88736-175-7.

Tate, Claudia. "Alice Walker." In *Black Women Writers at Work.* Ed. by Claudia Tate. New York: Continuum Press, 1983. pp. 175-187. LC: 82-23546. ISBN: 0-8264-0232-1.

Walker, Alice. "Writing *The Color Purple.*" In *In Search of Our Mother's Gardens; Womanist Prose.* New York: Harcourt, Brace, Jovanovich, 1983. pp. 355-360. LC: 83-8584. ISBN: 0-15-144525-7.

Awards and Prizes

American Book Award for Fiction, 1983.
Pulitzer Prize for Fiction, 1983.

Recommended Reading Lists

Books for You: A Booklist for Senior High Students. Ed. by Donald R. Gallo. Committee on the Senior High Booklist, Urbana, IL: National Council of Teachers of English, 1985. pp. 98, 334. LC: 85-21666. ISBN: 0-8141-0363-4.

Fiction Catalog, 11th Ed. Ed. by Juliette Yaakov. New York: H. W. Wilson, 1986. p. 637. LC: 85-32298. ISBN: 0-8242-0728-9.

My Darling, My Hamburger

By Paul Zindel

New York: Harper and Row, 1969. LC: 70-85025. ISBN: 0-06-026823-9.

Annotation

Paul Zindel tries to write not about how teenagers experience life, but as teens themselves might express their experience of life. This approach could be a carryover from his theatrical work to his fiction, since it is not unusual for a playwright to talk through his characters rather than talking about them.

When he is most successful, there is an urgency about his characters, a real sense of how desperately in a hurry they are to grow up, or at least to be treated as grown up, even when they least act like it. When Zindel is successful---as he is successful in *My Darling, My Hamburger*---the immediacy of his characters overcomes even the quaint slang and the out-of-date prices ($38 for a prom dress, $75 a month to rent an apartment, $300 for an illegal abortion).

It's not that Zindel recalls so well what it felt like to be seventeen. Rather, he can still feel that way, and he can put those feelings into the stumbling, self-conscious, semi-articulate words of a seventeen-year-old, who doesn't know who he is or what she wants yet, but does know who he doesn't want to be or what she isn't willing to settle for.

In *My Darling, My Hamburger* Zindel contrasts two young couples in their senior year of high school. Liz and Sean, rebelling against distant and self-absorbed parents, tumble head-over-heels into an accidental pregnancy that ends in abortion. Maggie and David, though equally unsure of themselves, are less miserable at home because they are not left so completely to fend for themselves. Consequently, they are able to find the strength to suffer through their present uncertainty and wait for better times to come. By the book's end, they feel stronger, sadder but wiser, and better able to cope with the world waiting beyond high school.

In a word, Zindel is counseling his readers to slow down. He attempts to show them that if they will take life slowly, be patient with themselves and the people around them, no matter how rushed and overwhelmed they may feel, they will get through their growing up time better in the long run. He offers no happily-ever-afters, but gives a sense of the real satisfactions that come from self-worth.

Examples of Recent Challenges

Removed from the Frazee, Minnesota school library (1973); from the Lyons, New York Elementary School library (1976); from the Hiawatha, Iowa Public Library (1979).

Challenged in Champaign, Illinois (1980) and Jefferson County, Kentucky (1982).

Source: The Office for Intellectual Freedom, American Library Association.

Reviews

Commonweal. 91:257 (11/21/69). ISSN: 0010-3330.

Library Journal. 94:4303 (11/15/69). ISSN: 0363-0277.

New York Times Book Review. (11/9/69). ISSN: 0028-7806.

Standard Reference Sources

Children's Literature Review. Ed. by Gerald J. Senick. Detroit: Gale Research Company, 1978. v.3 pp. 244-254. LC: 75-34953. ISBN: 0-8103-0079-6.

Contemporary Literary Criticism. Ed. by Jean C. Stine. Detroit: Gale Research Company, 1983. v.26 pp. 470-481. LC: 76-38938. ISBN: 0-8103-4400-9.

Current Biography Yearbook/1973. Ed. by Charles Moritz. New York: H. W. Wilson, 1974. pp. 445-448. LC: 40-27432. ISBN 0-8242-0543-X.

Something About the Author. Ed. by Anne Commire. Detroit: Gale Research Company, 1979. v.16 pp. 283-290. LC: 72-27107. ISBN: 0-8103-0097-4.

Twentieth Century Children's Writers, 2nd Ed. Ed. by D. L. Kirkpatrick. New York: St. Martin's Press, 1983. pp. 853-854. LC: 83-40062. ISBN: 0-312-82414-9.

Who's Who in America; 1986-1987, 44th Ed. 2v. Wilmette, IL: Marquis Who's Who/Macmillan Directory Division, 1986. v.2 p. 3073. LC: 4-16934. ISBN: 0-8379-0144-8.

Articles

Eaglen, Audrey. "Of life, love, death, kids and inhalation therapy: an interview with Paul Zindel." *Top of the News* 34:178-185 (Winter/78). ISSN: 0040-9286.

Haley, Beverly A. and Kenneth L. Donelson. "Pigs and hamburgers, cadavers and gamma rays: Paul Zindel's adolescents." *Elementary English* 51:940-945 (10/74). ISSN: 0013-5968.

Janeczko, Paul. "Interview with Paul Zindel." *English Journal* 66:20-21 (10/77). ISSN: 0013-8274.

Peck, Richard. "In the country of teenage fiction." *American Libraries* 4:204-207 (4/73). ISSN: 0002-9769.

Miscellaneous Discussion

Henke, James T. "Six characters in search of the family: the novels of Paul Zindel." *Young Adult Literature: Background and Criticism*. Compiled by Millicent Lenz and Ramona M. Mahood. Chicago: American Library Association, 1980. pp. 132-141. LC: 80-23489. ISBN: 0-8389-0302-9.

Rees, David. "Viewed from a squashed eyeball: Paul Zindel." In *The Marble in the Water: Essays on Contemporary Writers of Fiction for Children and Young Adults*. Boston: Hornbook, 1980. pp. 25-35. LC: 80-16623. ISBN: 0-87675-2-80-6.

Awards and Prizes

Pulitzer Prize for Drama, 1971 for "The Effect of Gamma Rays on Man-in-the-Moon Marigolds."

Recommended Reading Lists

Carlsen, G. Robert. *Books and the Teenage Reader, 2nd Revised Ed*. New York: Harper and Row, 1980. p. 76. LC: 78-2117. ISBN:0-06-010626-3.

Junior High School Catalog, 4th Ed. Ed. by Gary L. Bogart and Richard H. Isaacson. New York: H. W. Wilson, 1980. p. 458. LC: 80-53462. ISBN: 0-8242-0652-5.

Reading Ladders for Human Relations, 5th Ed. Ed. by Virginia M. Reid. Committee on Reading Ladders for Human Relations. National Council of Teachers of English. Washington, DC: American Council on Education, 1972. p. 79. LC: 72-87462. ISBN: 0-8268-1375-5.

Wilkin, Binnie Tate. *Survival Themes in Fiction for Children and Young People*. Metuchen, NJ: Scarecrow Press, 1978. p. 59. LC: 77-14295. ISBN: 0-8108-1048-4.

Senior High School Library Catalog, 13th Ed. New York: H. W. Wilson, 1987. LC: 87-7377. ISBN: 0-8242-0755-6.

Record of Challenges

Both the Office for Intellectual Freedom, American Library Association, and The People for the American Way keep and publish a record of the number of challenges reported to their respective offices. The numbers in the following list represent the challenges reported to the OIF between September 1979 and December 1986 and to the People for the American Way between 1982-1987.

Titles	*OIF*	*People*
Judy Blume. *Deenie.*	22	7
Boston Women's Health Collective. *Our Bodies, Ourselves.*	16	2
Judy Blume. *Forever.*	15	6
Anonymous. *Go Ask Alice.*	10	7
Robert Cormier. *The Chocolate War.*	9	9
John Steinbeck. *Of Mice and Men.*	9	8
Shirley Jackson. *The Lottery.*	9	2
Mark Twain. *The Adventures of Huckleberry Finn.*	7	7
J. D. Salinger. *The Catcher in the Rye.*	6	8
Katherine Paterson. *The Great Gilly Hopkins.*	4	2
Sandra Scoppettone. *Happy Endings Are All Alike.*	4	1
William Golding. *Lord of the Flies.*	4	2
Frances Hanckel and John Cunningham. *A Way of Love, A Way of Life.*	4	2
Daniel Keyes. *Flowers for Algernon.*	4	4
Kurt Vonnegut. *Slaughterhouse Five.*	4	3
Paul Zindel. *My Darling, My Hamburger.*	3	1
Robert Newton Peck. *A Day No Pigs Would Die.*	3	1
Alice Walker. *The Color Purple.*	3	4
Stephen King. *Cujo.*	2	5
Harry Mazer. *The Last Mission.*	2	1